how-to
'KILL'
THE MOCKING
BIRDS?

HOW-TO 'KILL' THE MOCKING BIRDS?

BRUCE NELSON

BRIDGEWOOD PUBLISHING
An Imprint of Cedar Fort, Inc.
Springville, Utah

ISBN 13: 9781462142835

Published by Bridgewood Publishing, an imprint of Cedar Fort, Inc.
2373 W. 700 S., Springville, UT 84663

Printed in the United States of America

10 9 8 7 6 5 4 3 2 1

Printed on acid-free paper

CONTENTS

DEDICATION

"Where none shall come to hurt or make afraid."

—William Clayton, 1846.

(Memoirs of some meek and especially
sincere pre-LDS investigations.)

Of course, I love and **dedicate** this book to the idea of lasting family-unity; to our five children and seven grandchildren; to all great wisdom, music, and literature ever uplifting our spirits and our lives. Also, more than anything else...

...I **dedicate** this book to my wife Janet (and her sister Lynn), whose heroic and patient 'underdog' story I am forever honored to tell. They are shining examples for all of us, especially the most *vulnerable and innocent* amongst us who have been wrongfully blamed, hurt, shamed, labeled, 'gaslighted', or even mildly marginalized, as willing or ironic 'victims' or 'fools' of their own struggles.

Please see - The Epilogue - at the very end of this book. Where Janet and I pledge to **dedicate** as much promotion and profits from this book as we possibly can towards helping those struggling *alone or single*, with any mis-diagnosed -- mis-treated -- or any and every isolated, trivialized, marginalized, *homeless* or misunderstood mental or spiritual struggles. Especially any developmental or other disabilities, eating disorders, mental illness or breakdowns due to PTSD.

DISCLAIMER

OF OUR PERSONAL AND GLOBAL STRUGGLES IN FAITH, UNITY, AND COMMON SENSE

The views and opinions expressed herein are mine alone. This subject is much bigger and broader than me, you, or even America in general. And, although I include examples of outrageous intolerance and disharmony from current politics and religion, I definitely do not intend to mock or judge anyone's best ideals or values, or to present this disharmony as hopeless, or my only important focus or purpose. That, sadly and ironically, might actually foster even more fear and intolerance than we apparently already have here.

THE PROLOGUE

"LISTEN TO THE MOCKINGBIRDS"

"Hush, little baby don't say a word. Papa's gonna buy you a **Mockingbird**."

—from Mother Goose Rhymes,
the actual author is unknown.

Mockingbirds are symbols of vulnerable innocence. Perhaps, they can also be heroic, triumphant symbols of genuine patience and courage to stand strong in the face of pushy and intolerant mocking, scoffing, gaslighting naysayers. Symbols of fighting back with healing, patience, gentleness, kindness, with moral-ethical leadership and irony (i.e. 'killing' with patience and kindness). With the kind of 'Biblical' irony that literally "cuts both ways", and with "sharpness".

"How-to" books and videos have been increasing tremendously, using innovative formats like "for Dummies" and YouTube tutorial "video-shorts". But nobody, at least that I know of, has ever used a "how-to" title -- by metaphorically and ironically referring and linking it to any significant Pulitzer prize winning materials, or titles. Nonetheless, I will hereby attempt to do so.

> "Mockingbirds don't do one thing but make music for us to enjoy . . . but sing their hearts out for us. That's why it's a sin to kill a mockingbird."
>
> —Harper Lee, *To Kill a Mockingbird.*

Before publishing and finally promoting her classic novel, Harper Lee assisted her childhood friend Truman Capote during his extensive interviews and notes for his non-fiction novel, *"In Cold Blood"*. She had already written her novel's first draft in the mid-1950s (later, this draft was published in 2015 against her long-standing wishes and intentions, as the fraudulently-supposed sequel to *To Kill a Mockingbird, "Go Set a Watchman"*).

During interviews, Capote kept insisting (against Harper's cautions) that he could succeed at the innovative and insightful use of difficult triple narrative describing the lives of the murderers, the victims, and other members of the rural community in alternating sequences within his eloquent true crime novel. One can only speculate about how these struggles might have helped inspire Harper's finishing touches on her best-selling book *"To Kill a Mockingbird"*.

> "Real courage is when you know you're licked before you begin, but you begin anyway and see it through no matter what."
>
> —Harper Lee, *To Kill a Mockingbird.*

Harper Lee clearly uses Mockingbirds metaphorically, possibly referring to innocent underdogs, such as Arthur "Boo" Radley, Tom Robinson (a scapegoat), Scout, or even "Dill" Harris (who was patterned after Capote).

Harper Lee significantly refers to the social and cultural hierarchies (especially woven upon complex hypocrisies and denials) within her fictional little Southern city of Maycomb, Alabama in the 1930s, including the surrounding county of the same name. I think we are all plenty smart enough to recognize many similar hierarchies, hypocrisies, and denialisms in the modern societies and cultures within which we each live and work today.

I believe that the subtle but intolerant uses of "mocking," "zingers," and "gaslighting" denialisms against everyone (but especially against our most vulnerable underdogs) have grown exponentially in our current modern culture to become serious problems. But these are also serious new opportunities for us to learn, understand, and fix some things, if we can find the authentic, genuine courage and patience to do so.

Please explore the many shared metaphors and patterns within the stories included in this book. I sincerely hope you find even more ideas here than those that I intended to include. I have tried hard to include even more different and significant links, ironies and metaphoric patterns to heroic/innocent underdogs, scapegoats, and "mockingbirds" than those created within Harper Lee's award-winning novel, and its subsequent Oscar winning movie.

Civil courage links (i.e. ethics or morals) to the title *In Cold Blood* would be particularly relevant today, given the amount of 'cold-blooded' intolerant mocking, scoffing, bullying, or denialism seen so often nowadays (including the quiet, pretending acts of looking the other way). And, the somehow ever growing exaggerated rumors and gossip based upon extreme theories and half-truths.

Since I mention the intolerance of politics, religions, or other forms of leadership so prominently, many will assume that is my main purpose and audience. However, since those leading and participating in such intolerance are so unlikely to hearken to or acknowledge these stories, my main purpose, hope, and audience are actually the various vulnerable underdogs themselves, and those who care the most about them. Thus, I hope these stories can empower them to heal and find more genuine patience towards intolerance, and to boldly move forward with even greater courage and conviction than ever before. Because despite being so beaten-down and trivialized, true underdogs are very often vastly underestimated.

In other words, I want to inspire but also help the most vulnerable scapegoats and any other innocent underdogs or "mockingbirds". I want to help them NOT get hurt or 'killed' so much. To stop the hurting of the vulnerable underdogs, sometimes we need to learn more about 'killing' the pushy Mockers back a little, not in violence or revenge; rather 'killing or healing them with patience and kindness'.

Bullying always stops (at least for a while) when "bystanders" combine to carefully document and report it in some way, or maybe even courageously or creatively "intervene" in some other significant way. Kindness is free, always kill'em with kindness.

CONCERNING "BYSTANDER APATHY", OR DENIALISM OF HARM AND ABUSE FROM BULLYING:

- STOP bystander fear, apathy, and denials of harm and abuse.
- STOP any kind of "by-standing for bullies".
- Intervene, Document & Report them ALL.
  - » Always include those closest bystanders.

- Realize that the initial stopping of it is not enough.
  - » Accountability and healing that lasts takes more time, effort, and especially patience.
  - » Healing is critical for all parties:
    - – victims, perps, and closest bystanders.
    - – Kindness is free, so "kill'em all with kindness".

CONCERNING THE GROWING PREVALENCE FOR "LEARNED HELPLESSNESS" AND "ENABLED" APATHY, ADDICTIONS, AND OTHER UN-NECESSARY DYSFUNCTIONS WITHIN OUR CULTURE.

Such "helplessness" and apathy can be effectively reduced, as repeatedly proven within many "disability" groupings. But, it is a serious growing problem in many modern families, communities, and coddled individuals whenever it is hidden or denied. Our shared modern culture seems to have lots of problems with such apathy, "learned helplessness", and dysfunctional behaviors related to bullying, addictions, anxiety, depression, phobias, stressors, and denialism. Kindness is free, always kill'em with kindness.

Growing up in northern Minnesota, I had never actually seen or heard a mockingbird. So early one Saturday morning after moving to

Greensboro, NC my wife Janet woke me saying, "Listen, do you know what that is? It's a mockingbird going through his repertoire of sounds." Sure enough we soon discovered a nest built deep into a thick Quince-bush with long sharp thorns everywhere. Those mockingbirds continued to use that bush each year that we lived there.

Our next door neighbors had a fat old cat that would lay in the shade beside their car sitting in the driveway. Several times we observed our two crafty mockingbirds go underneath the neighbor's car to torment that old cat by picking at his tail or other areas of his fur. It was such entertainment keeping up with those two very feisty, spunky mockingbirds.

Soon after Janet's divorce, she needed employment to support herself and her two daughters. Her teaching certifications had lapsed, but she found temporary employment on several big educational testing projects as a reader of essay responses to generic literacy prompts.

Janet never dreamed back then that she would ever find a connection to a real future book title. But, in one of the tested states, the students had studied Harper Lee's "To Kill a Mockingbird" that year, and so were prompted to respond to that book. Many of the responses were quite surprising (and funny), including those who incorrectly remembered the title as: *"HOW to kill a Mockingbird"*, *"The Killer Mockingbird"*, and even *"Blues* (Boo?) *ain't no Mockingbird"*.

I can testify that this book and title are no coincidence. Many heroes, angels, miracles, and tender mercies have come forth to bring it to pass. It has brought us hidden treasures of peace and comfort, to both mind and soul. And, it can bring the same to you and yours, if you give it half a chance.

OF MOCKING, AND MOCKERS.

During the Civil War, President Abraham Lincoln was especially fond of hearing the then popular ballad "Listen to the Mocking Bird", by Septimus Winner, selling over twenty million copies of sheet music over its various publishings beginning in 1855. Lincoln said, "It is as sincere as the laughter of a little girl at play." Even though the ballad tells of a mockingbird singing over a sweetheart's grave, Septimus Winner sold several different publications and printings all using the two separated words, "Mocking - Bird", in the title instead of the expected spelling of "Mockingbird".

I think that title-oddity might be significant given the prevalence of "mocking" in our culture and throughout history, especially before and during the US Civil War, but you decide for yourself. Septimus Winner also wrote and published the nursery-songs "Oh where, oh where has my little dog gone?" and "Ten Little Injuns" with political-satire hidden within the words, and the song Sweet Ellie Rhee (or "Carry me back to Tennessee"). He also used pseudonyms in referring to himself in the credits of his publications for unknown reasons. He used the pseudonym Alice Hawthorne in his first publication of "Listen to the Mocking Bird".

We all seem to vastly underestimate and sometimes "mock" many of the most courageously different lives, ideas, imagined-dreams, and people found scattered randomly and mercifully amongst us. Until many of us are just a bit too fearful to ever really live or feel anything dangerously different or genuinely divine for ourselves at all.

DISILLUSIONMENT OF TEN O'CLOCK

– from Harmonium: Poetry by Wallace Stevens.

The houses are haunted
By white night-gowns.
None are green,
Or purple with green rings,
Or green with yellow rings,
Or yellow with blue rings.
None of them are strange,
With socks of lace
And beaded ceintures.
People are not going
To dream of baboons and periwinkles.
Only, here and there, an old sailor,
Drunk and asleep in his boots,
Catches tigers
In red weather.

PART 0

INTRODUCTION

OF TRUE FRIENDSHIPS, LEADERSHIP, AND CITIZENSHIP.

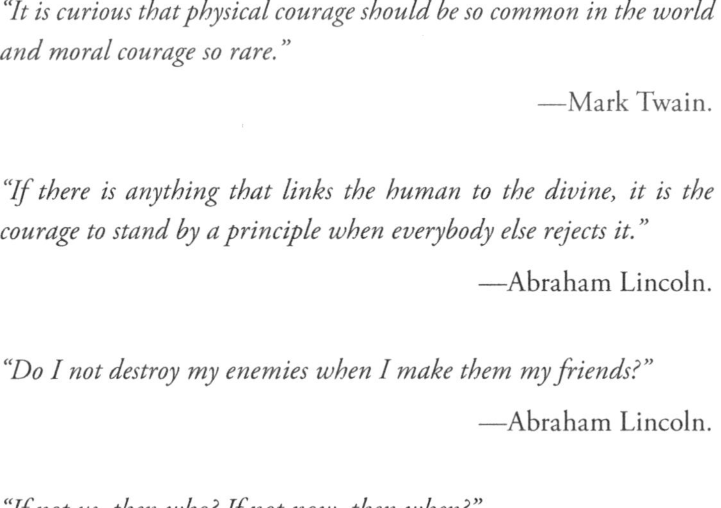

"It is curious that physical courage should be so common in the world and moral courage so rare."

—Mark Twain.

"If there is anything that links the human to the divine, it is the courage to stand by a principle when everybody else rejects it."

—Abraham Lincoln.

"Do I not destroy my enemies when I make them my friends?"

—Abraham Lincoln.

"If not us, then who? If not now, then when?"

—John Lewis (also Rabbi Hillel the Elder c. 110 BCE).

THE IMPORTANCE OF FINDING AND TELLING OUR OWN PERSONAL STORIES.

"Knowing others is intelligence; knowing yourself is true wisdom."

—Lao Tzu.

Finding, choosing, and acting with true and independent moral courage is a rare, valuable, and heroic aspect of human nature. Rare, because most of us get caught up in groups defined by somebody else's narrative, then somehow remain caught. Oh, we jump back and forth between the various groups whenever we want or decide, and we always possess our own 'voices' inside these groups. But, we seldom seem to find, heal, or create our own independent narrative.

Listen, and hear; if we don't find, act, and tell our own stories (narratives), who else will? And likewise, if we don't actively listen and hear the others needing to be heard, nobody will ever know or really care much about our most important struggles or inner feelings, truths, and strengths.

"Your time is limited, so don't waste it living someone else's life."

—Steve Jobs.

Again, most of us impatiently and repeatedly get recruited and caught up in various popular group identities and concerns (or "collectivist group-narratives"), such as exclusive in-group vs. out-group identities, concerns, and politics. We do this rather than really healing and finding our own inner peace, truth, and strengths. We can even mistakenly start to lose our own personal stories or identities, and our own inner moral courage.

Some have compared ancient and modern evidence, and found that hidden deep within every culture and person lies a somewhat universal but dormant desire for heroic "dream-quests" (see *"The Hero with a Thousand Faces"* by Joseph Campbell). We all seem attracted to and resonate towards such deeply embedded ideals when we hear the many similar stories and myths of heroes and their brave journeys and quests. This book will explore such in general terms; but will also encourage you to explore and ponder such within yourself.

We all serve sometimes as part-time heroes, mentors, or friends to someone else (as pseudo life-coaches?). But it's much harder - and rarer - to independently be a "best" hero, mentor, or friend to ourselves. Everyone struggles and suffers hurts and pains. None of us leaves this life without experiencing the deep sting of "dusty" death. But nobody's struggles are exactly the same. We can't be our best selves. And we can't be the best heroes, mentors, and friends to others, until we can become such to ourselves.

BE THE BEST VERSION OF YOU.

"We must not allow other people's limited perceptions to define us."

—Virginia Satir

"Owning our story and loving ourselves through that process is the bravest thing we'll ever do."

—Brené Brown

"One of the greatest regrets in life is being what others would want you to be, rather than being yourself."

—Shannon L. Alder

I am not suggesting that your personal "quests" should be quick, do-it-yourself journeys, or filled with complaining "righteous revenge" or angry payback (much like the so-so heroes in Hollywood action-thrillers, or popular self-help fads). Conversely, we find that within the greatest heroes and quests, although self-reliance and a strong sense of self-responsibility are always key characteristics, complete isolation of effort without any divine outside help, healing, or guidance, is never part of those most important and successful quests.

Although temptations for revenge, and quick, popular solutions are usually present, the true courageous hero usually concludes that the longer, slower, more patient way turns out to be the best for the lasting success and unity of everyone. Often such patience is accompanied by mocking, scoffing, and bullying, but always leads them to the better victory.

The trouble is, we seldom seem to find enough genuine courage or patience to start, own, or further our own personal "dream-quests." We're usually too comfortable, and just a little too scared, to take the risk, to try, to change, or even to consider "really" seeing things from the long run, or from any other perspectives. Especially if that perspective or person is seen or considered a chronic underdog, or more especially, a foolish or vulnerable scapegoat.

Surely, America has had a great run of wealth and success, and I love the "American Dream" that has inspired so many of us. Yet, most now see it seriously sinking into a perpetual and divisive sea of tribal disharmony and denialisms. So I am writing these stories and ideas as my personal witness and example that "The BEST is Yet to be." I hope, as well, that it can help lasting truth and harmony be a possibility within your personal story, too.

Even though this book mentions the "tribal disharmony" of extreme politics and religion today, please do not react negatively or take offense. That is not my focus or purpose. Whichever end of the extreme political or religious spectrum you might feel closest to is totally okay! Let's all just try to be a little more careful, more thoughtful, more understanding, and not so quick to throw the proverbial "baby" (items of importance and value) out with the bathwater.

I hope we can try respectfully listening to each other's highest hopes and ideals, whether we agree totally, or not. I hope we can carefully hear and understand each other's best plans and objectives. I hope we can refrain from questioning the private inner-faith or patriotism of others.

I hope we can bravely own our actions and struggles, and take adequate personal responsibility for the problems and difficulties around us, instead of complaining and blaming others who have contradicting ideas. Then, maybe, we have a chance to avoid and heal some of the disharmony and gridlock that we are currently stuck in.

As you read the stories and examples in this book, please take some time to quietly ponder your own inner truths and strengths; your own personal story. I believe that the stories and examples in this book will help you gain a new perspective on yourself and others around you.

And thus maybe start writing your own stories. Everyone's story and struggles are important; More important than any of us now know. So start writing or recording your own, or your closest loved one's important stories and struggles. This book is living proof that you can do it, and that you will never regret starting and even struggling at recording them. Because the uniquely hardest struggles are always the most interesting and important parts. And it's always therapeutic for any of us to seriously ponder and write about them.

> *"No man is an island, entire of itself; every man is a piece of the continent, a part of the main. If a clod be washed away by the sea, Europe is the less, as well as if a promontory were, as well as if a manor of thy friend's or of thine own were: any man's death diminishes me, because I am involved in mankind, and therefore never send to know for whom the bell tolls; it tolls for thee."*
>
> —An honored quote about genuine, inclusive unity,
> by John Donne from *Devotions upon*
> *Emergent Occasions* (1623), XVII.

CHAPTER 1

THE MAN WHO MARRIED JANET JONES.

Much of this book covers some extraordinarily compelling stories about my wife, Janet. After we married over 27 years ago, I would hear people whisper, "He's the man who married Janet Jones." So, for a while I would actually introduce myself with; "Yes, I'm the man who married Janet Jones."

You see, although these people only knew a very small portion of the incredible stories and journeys that will be included within these pages. Many of them had already recognized that there was something uniquely special but strangely hidden about this seemingly ordinary woman, Janet Jones.

For example, everyone knows that 1 + 1 = 2. But, in certain special cases like the greatest artworks, music, and literature, 1 + 1 somehow boldly ends up equaling more. If you continue reading here, look for those subtle and unexpected extras beyond the rational or merely physical. Because that's what is hoped for and intended, that you might find these unexpected ideas and "extras" within these stories and journeys, and within yourselves.

It takes genuine courage and patience for anyone to really find yourself, your purpose, your truth, and your own independent story, especially if your story has the suppressed, gaslighted underdog elements of Janet's story. Thus, this book is also a story about me searching and finding the courage and perseverance to carefully hear and write Janet's somewhat unspeakable (and much misunderstood) underdog story. In doing so, I had to take on risks and perilous hardships to explore and learn much about myself. This included my most elusive subconscious thoughts, memories, hypocrisies, and weaknesses. It touched my deep inner core, my most private inner spirit and even my elusive immortal soul.

Yet, this book is about much more than just Janet, or me, or these personal stories. It's about the possibilities and blessings of true and genuine courage and sacrifice, beyond which most are willing to go.

All of us can help each other to find and foster those blessings and possibilities of courage and service towards ourselves and others, together, within this book. They are the soft, subtle blessings of true peace, comfort, and freedom to think, ponder, choose, and act for yourself (separate from any pushy collectivist group or thinking).

I believe if you quietly ponder upon these ideas you will be able to recognize, understand more, and seek after this 'voice' within yourself. Others have called it your inner conscience or intuition, your common sense, your inner "still small voice", your guardian-angel, the Holy Spirit within you, or the Holy Ghost. It is never immoral, unethical, "loud", or pushy. In fact, unless you patiently seek it independently, you might never find it or ever feel, sense, or 'hear' it at all. The stories in this book will likewise attempt to help you understand, and listen, better to this quiet voice.

The thing nobody can tell you is exactly how, when, or where it will come for you. It's usually not an "audible" voice for me, more like uniquely "flavored" bursts of thoughts, feelings, or promptings that are original enough that I can innocently tell they didn't originate simply with me. Thus, they must have come from a higher source and intelligence.

It's a bit different each time, and different for everyone. So, only *you* can find that one out for yourself, friend. Only you.

Yet, many of us sometimes tend to sit-back and lean on the examples and testimonies of those around us. Listen, ...that is a lazy and irresponsible way to base our personal or spiritual faith, so let's all try something more than that. Keep reading here for new ideas and encouragements to get you started.

There are many different types and shades of courage. This book is about that most special and rare type of courage. I believe it's the type that makes Janet so special and rare. Let's call it "moral courage" -- to patiently stand for important personal values and ethics, no matter how mocked, bullied, or unpopular they might be. Not to take offense, or to be offended by such. Not to resist any efforts or hope of mending any such offenses, or rifts with others.

Conversely, such is the courage to patiently *never* take offense, and to *always* stay open to mending any rifts or offenses. Kindness is free, so always kill'em with kindness, and patience.

This is almost always, in some way, inspired or assisted by the kind examples and Graces of God, or those subtle-elusive inner promptings from a hidden and higher Heaven; whether we recognize and fully understand them or not.

Please keep reading, so we can help you explore and find more of this soft, but long lasting gentle peace and comfort.

> *"Sometimes you have to lose yourself 'fore you can find anything."*
>
> —Lewis (Burt Reynolds) in "Deliverance."

> *"He that findeth his life shall lose it: and he that loseth his life for my sake shall find it."*
>
> —Matt 10:39 KJV.

SEVERAL COMMON-SENSE PERSPECTIVES VS. THE CONSTANT DISHARMONY AND GRIDLOCK COMING FROM TODAY'S ANGRY POLITICAL AND RELIGIOUS ELITES.

Examples: A tale of two families: Lifestyles of the very rich, the famous, and the super-spoiled.

Recently, a somewhat immature but royal young prince and his celebrity wife did a "shocking" press interview to complain about incessant mocking in the powerful tabloid journalism media. They explained that because these tabloids need access to royals to sell and survive, the mocking could have been easily and effectively stopped or decreased through the existing agreements between the top-royals and those tabloids.

But, because his young wife was an American entertainment-celebrity divorcee and bi-racial, she was cruelly and deliberately not protected. And when feelings of chronic anxiety and suicide resulted, her pleas for help or therapy were ignored. The young Prince further explained that his dad and brother are miserably trapped and bullied by a "cult-like" system of executive secretaries that restrict and run every top royal's affairs.

A former U.S. President, whose long-term personal lawyer recently went to prison for bribes and tampering in lawsuits involving such tabloid media, predicted that the "fairytale status" of this young Prince and his bride would eventually be completely destroyed by the hypocrisy and corruption within these systems.

It's important to consider here that this former President was also born into elite status and wealth. He is famous for often accusing and labeling the mainstream media as "fake news". Yet, he repeatedly tweeted, started, or promoted extreme lies, half-truths, and exaggerated theories about his opponents and even about unproven and supposedly conspired U.S. election voting fraud, casting serious doubts on U.S. voting results, integrity, security, checks, audits, and our entire U.S. election voting systems as a whole.

According to several respected fact-checking services, no Western leader in recorded history has ever come close to his frequency or proficiency for "officially" bending the truth. Yet, many leading megachurch televangelists repeatedly and effectively defended him and his truth-defying tactics as justified in the name of more readily and finally winning the political culture war against the "liberal-leaning press", as well as the "dangerous elite secular globalists and socialists" (collectivist ideologies). So, are they telling us that in this case *"the Ends do justify the Means?"* Or maybe they mean, *"It's okay as long as you don't get caught, or convicted?"* Please decide for yourself about these questions.

I do not want or intend to judge anyone in these stories. I surely do not intend to question anyone's private inner-faith or patriotism. This book is not actually about spoiled or whining celebrities, churches, or politics. I'm sure you have your own favorite opinions and interpretations on these particular celebrity stories, as you should. But, I have included them within this opening chapter, only to briefly illustrate and demonstrate the flavor and kind of stories (about genuine patience and courage vs. counterfeit, faked, or façaded bravery), and how they might relate to modern moral courage, that I will be sharing within the discussions of this book.

Verbal "zingers", whether mere blaming, complaining, and bickering (or other more vengeful protestations like serious and damaging rumors and gossip based upon exaggerations, lies, or half-truths), eventually hurt everyone enough to damage even the most important personal and civic relationships in our lives and our communities.

The courage to patiently stand firm for ourselves and our independent truths and beliefs is an important progression we all need to make in our development of a fullness of personal independence from the status quo. Exaggerated or pushy false bluster, counterfeit courage, or faked positivity often influences or intimidates many of us, and can sometimes bring shallow short term victory or wins. But will never bring the lasting results, nor the peace of mind or soul that true and sincere moral courage and patience can bring.

I believe -- I *choose* to believe -- that even the crushed "fairytale" dreams of the young royal Prince, and the exaggerating ex-President (and his many personal lawyers and followers) can still be mended. And, that if we can return to careful and respectful listening to each other, that almost any relationship breach can yet be improved, if not totally repaired.

A MORE COMMON SENSE PERSPECTIVE.

A wise old proverbial toast says:

> *"There are TALL ships and small ships, and ships that sail the seas.*
> *But if the best ships are friendships, then cheers to you and me."*
>
> —Author unknown.

I think most everybody can agree with this toast. Within our life's many pathways the good and true friendships we manage to find and keep are maybe the best parts of the journey. And, that the very best friendships are built upon inter-dependent loyalty, effective listening skills, healthy respect and communications; not in words only, but proven more assuredly through actions, including consistent and caring acts of kindness, dignity, and devotion.

For example: The lasting inter-dependent friendship and help between Harper Lee and Truman Capote that produced the two precious and award winning novels mentioned earlier, in The Prologue.

Besides friendships, several other very important "ships" along these journeys are: good and true citizen*ship*, leader*ship*, and our spousal-relation*ships*. Interestingly, the best of these are also built upon *"inter-dependent loyalty, effective listening skills, healthy respect and communications; not in words only, but proven more assuredly through actions, including consistent and caring acts of kindness, dignity, and devotion."*

For example: The courageous and noble citizenship between lawyer Atticus Finch, Sheriff Heck Tate, and the vulnerable and disabled poor and black families in Harper Lee's beloved novel.

Since we seem to be having unusual evidences (and numbers) of disrespectful and unkind breakdowns, meltdowns, and divisiveness in the quality of the citizenship and leadership (even some family relationships and friendships) that are coming forth lately, I decided to appeal to everybody's common sense and common knowledge about friendships, citizenship, and leadership as models for comparison, and for looking forward to possible personal and group improvements.

My common sense tells me that a serious lack of genuine and independent moral courage is a growing factor in these disrespectful and unkind breakdowns (filled with complaining and blaming). Instead of bravely owning our actions and struggles, and taking adequate personal responsibility for the problems and difficulties around us, we're getting too distracted by exclusive in-group vs. out-group identities, and by angry "identity politics."

And, I believe that this lack of moral courage is making all of us more vulnerable to getting recruited and caught up within these 'cultish' and tribal identity groups and politics. For example, enough of the cheap, easy, shallow, and watered-down friendships, citizenship, leadership, and loud petty-grievances we see today in so many of our relationships. We need more of those truly courageous *"ships"*. Kindness is free, so kill'em with kindness.

Most of these modern/postmodern identity group movements and leaders do not encourage or emphasize nearly enough of patiently and heroically owning our struggles and taking personal responsibility for the problems and difficulties around us. It's always quicker, easier, and more popular to militantly take offense, to complain or blame, and to recruit and promote big, popular tribal rallies (even though most go along mostly to observe, as "bystanders"). We tend to blame and shame supposed cultural enemies (or other vulnerable scapegoats) for most of our struggles and problems, and even our personal struggles and difficulties. It's always much harder and takes much longer to "be the change that you wish to see in the world" (Mohandas Gandhi), or to stop allowing so much easily accepted "bystander apathy" within ourselves or others.

> *"Change will not come if we wait for some other person, or if we wait for some other time. We are the ones we've been waiting for.* ***We are the change that we seek."***
>
> —Barack Obama.

The angry protests, attacks, and fighting words even seem to make some feel a sort of snobbish fake courage. For example, independent stands against simple, common sense public health suggestions or *mandates* (like quarantines, vaccines, masks, or distancing) may seem courageous, and even patriotic (for personal liberty). But, such immature bickering and blaming (especially when based upon possible inaccurate or misinformation) almost never produces any significant changes, neither any lasting peace of mind nor any lasting peace for our souls. And, such excessive complaining and blaming is certainly not good for our children to see, or take examples from.

I am not an elite expert on any of these social groups, issues, or trends. Thus, I do not intend to tell anyone else what they should think for themselves about these matters. Conversely, I simply intend to present some important and real life stories that demonstrate the need for a better way. These stories will support the positive notion that since struggles and sacrifice make us stronger; *"...so the BEST is yet to be"*. Please ponder these stories and notions for yourself, and discern what your common sense tells you.

UNIVERSAL YEARNINGS FOR 'UTOPIAN' UNITY.

Everyone yearns to belong, to be accepted, heard, and connected to others; especially in the most powerful traditions, rituals and culture (hence the enduring ideal of the perfect happy family, and community). Yet, we seem to be drowning in a modern/post-modern ocean of relationship anxiety and depression, addictions, divorce, domestic disloyalty and violence, mass shootings, bullying, and suicides. Not to mention, the recent international and worldwide wars, regional wars, cold wars, culture wars, cyber wars, and bigotry driven genocidal violence.

Social surveys and opinion-polling-data show people (especially youth) leaving their family's traditional churches, religion, and political positions in increasing numbers. Many for newer, more modern versions of their family's church. But, growing numbers are boldly choosing no organized religion or church affiliations. They seem fed-up, skeptical, or agnostic towards the legacies of unrighteous leadership, abusive corruption, hypocrisy, and/or greed. Their choices, based on overwhelming popular opinions, as more historical information, denials, and cover ups are revealed.

I love America. But it is far from perfect, yet. I especially love the many positive examples it has given to the rest of the world. Democracy is very messy, and never easy. Always has been, always will be. And yet, somehow, our vibrantly robust, mostly two-party system has regularly produced incredible successes and blessings to better the entire world. But, certainly not without many noble differences of opinions and viewpoints.

Note: I was warned not to try to "straddle the fence", or to try to respect and appeal to both sides within heated political views, or heated religious (or non-religious) viewpoints. I respectfully disagree. I am promoting true, genuine moral courage. The kind that never takes offense or gets offended. To demonstrate it is possible, I need to risk offending those still clutching to such worn-out, shallow, counterfeit, *failed*, and faked courage.

Out of respect to both sides, I sincerely hope you won't be offended, as I mention a few of these viewpoints, on both sides. All of which I consider valuable and positive. As proof of my understanding and respect, I offer the following summaries.

Briefly stated, and meaning no disrespect, left-wing (Liberal or Progressive) political groups tend to blame inherent greed and hypocrisies within the traditional and wealthy capitalist establishments. They point to evidences of systemic bigotry, racism, and sexism. They call for big government programs to help poor and working class people. They call for social justice and extensive economic programs and regulations to protect common people, such as with working conditions, welfare and medical, rent controls, and minimum wages. These 'liberal' groups are not overly concerned about losing youthful adherents, because their causes and voices almost always get plenty of popular coverage and positive support from academic elites and from mainstream media outlets. Yet, historic coalitions of liberal-causes are sometimes teetering, too expensive and diluted down to stand or stick together as much as they have in the past.

Right-wing (Conservative) political (and religious) groups often seem obsessively concerned about losing youthful adherents, because they claim unfair biased opposition coming from "radical" and "secular leaning" academic elites, career bureaucrats, and from the powerful liberal leaning influence of most Mainstream Media (MSM) outlets. They also blame these influences for diluting important "family values", the morals and ethics of "self-reliance", and other strong cultural traditions that have made America great, but are now somehow rapidly decreasing, and possibly disappearing.

Note: the brief summaries of political views and opinions, listed above, are not intended to be overly comprehensive or judgemental. I have included them, because I believe that all of these opinions and views are important, and have great and positive value; as long as they are not taken to overly pushy, dominant, mean-spirited, exaggerated, or loud radical extremes.

For instance, I support the importance and need for secular government (per U.S. Constitution: No established church or religion) as long as this secularism is not used or allowed to crush, silence, or gaslight spiritual feelings, personal faith, or artistry. I am a religionist, as long as one church, philosophy, or belief system (including secularism) is not allowed to suppress or bully others. Most of us see religion or churches as only those who worship divine entities. However, in this increasingly secular and modern, materialistic world of ours, many ordinary citizens today feel strongly that these new secular ideologies and philosophies are quickly becoming the new religious (or non-religious) bullies within our culture. And, thus as the newest and most currently favored "state religion" (despite their non-religion claim and status), they should at least be limited in how much they can infringe upon (or bully) any other church, religion, or philosophy.

I am all for free-market capitalism, as long as it is competently inspected and audited to prevent unfair advantage, especially to any extreme levels, as well as other corruptions or scams. The modern economy is far too complex for any ordinary citizens to fully understand and protect themselves alone without any help. Thus, we do need the various governments to help protect them and all of us from the most predatory bad-actors within this modern economic world of ours.

I am also a strong supporter of mainstream media's efforts and role in bringing fair and balanced journalistic reporting of the events, movements, and the politics around us, especially as an essential part of democracy, as much as they are reasonably able to.

Of course, media mergers have consolidated the ownership and power of these MSMs in the hands of a few rich and powerful people. And, of course some media bias is possible and even inevitable. However, if the well established professional journalistic standards and ethics are reviewed and reported as they mostly are today, I believe the civic truth can and will eventually be enough served within these media. Unfortunately, our modern info age is providing too many selfish and insensitive jerks -- unregulated access to many much-less professional tabloid news and opinion outlets, and informal/social media opportunities for extreme and exaggerated bias, un-regulated rumors, lies, and destructive gossip.

Very much like local police and public education, these MSMs play a great role and add value in our democracy and culture. All three of these important social entities are absolutely essential, since nobody else can or will fully fulfill those roles. Of course, given such huge, almost impossible roles, they will never be perfect in everything within those roles. But, since most are working hard together to produce the good, better, and best that they are able to provide, we need to listen and work together with them better, not always blaming them. Incidentally, they should never be unfairly or self-righteously judged or expected to always provide perfect, quick, or easy solutions just for you or anybody else, who for some hidden reasons are frustrated and can't seem to responsibly find their own personal truths, wisdom, choices, or their own individual story or purpose for themselves or their children.

Why then, given the problems and trends mentioned, do I think, *"the BEST is Yet to be"*? I think that the three important social entities mentioned here: local police, public education teachers, and the professional journalists working at MSMs (which now seemed to be so blamed and shamed by everybody) will again become seen as courageous heroes, especially given these most recent problems and trends. Yes, it will take some care and patience to get back there again.

ON MOCKING, AND MOCKERS

Our popular culture frequently demonstrates that we are, or should be, well aware of the amount of cynical mocking; And how very unproductive such chronic cynicism can be.

> *"We live in a cynical world. A cynical world! . . . You don't know what it's like to be me out here for you. It is an up-at-dawn, pride swallowing siege that I will never fully tell you about, ok?"*
>
> —Jerry Maguire, *"Jerry Maguire"*, 1996.

WE HAVE NOT COME THIS FAR; JUST TO COME THIS FAR... WE NEED TO FINISH ACHIEVING OUR ANCESTOR'S 'AMERICAN DREAMS'

The U.S.A. (and North America as a whole) has always seemed to attract and inspire some of the best (and worst) examples of moral courage. From the early explorers, pilgrims, and settlers to the inventors, entrepreneurs, entertainers, and scientists, America has always produced and inspired moral courage as well as crafty counterfeits. And America has always stepped up big-time during the very worst times and crises.

Most of us are immigrants. Either we, or our ancestors, courageously left a homeland behind, to seek and build a better future for ourselves and our posterity. Now, oddly we find ourselves drowning in a new modern world, over populated with an ocean of dissatisfied delinquents, who all seem to carry some angry and entitled protests, militantly complaining and blaming others for their struggles and difficulties. And, if by chance, they are not yet angry, they soon will be, no matter where on the political spectrum they may inhabit. Eventually, we all get somewhat caught up into some of the most popular political complaints, movements, opinions, or churches around us.

WE ARE LUCKY TO LIVE IN THE GREATEST AGE: THE INFO AGE.

Political negotiations for compromise is not a bad thing. In fact, if it is done carefully and with plenty of listening and understanding – it can be the noblest and best of things, especially at a time of such exaggerated political extremism and absolutism. Personally and politically, I am grateful for our American political democracy and legacies, even with all of its very worst-warts and weaknesses.

I have nothing against authentic, nonviolent civil resistance, that patiently, courageously, and gently teaches true principles, while also gently aiming at placing natural consequences towards any unjust oppression or hypocrisy until the oppressors come to realize their own mistaken policies. Not to punish, but rather to gently help them realize their own errors.

However, I don't see much of that kind of patient, nonviolent resistance happening anymore. Instead, we see counterfeits seeking a quick, easy, more popular version which always contains plenty of loud, biased complaining and blaming, and usually some exaggerated lies and bullying half-truths.

I have implied a link between hypocrisy and lack of moral courage. I have also mentioned organized religion in several examples of modern hypocrisy.

The major world religions all trace their origins back several thousand years, to ancient times. Each religion teaches that a common tendency for hypocrisy and sin exists within all of us, in every person, every leader, every group and nation, and especially the churches and religions.

Each major world religion teaches and provides numerous important examples that, because those same tendencies exist in leaders -- including religious leaders -- we are right to be wary of such hypocrisy. Thus, each major religion has documented and had repeated apostasies within, led by selfish leaders, corrupting group-influence for their own greed. Hence, the many wars and atrocities, both inside and outside these groups, influenced and partaken by these major religious groups and leaders.

Yet, the inherent needs and desires to change and improve have brought many reforms and restorations, always at great peril to any true and courageous reformer.

"Please don't shoot the messenger!"

Nevertheless, throughout recorded history the misled religious people have almost always rejected and 'stoned' their own best prophets and reformers, and so the long lists and legacies of so many courageous reformers and martyrs goes on. But, why does this happen so readily and so often?

Authentic patience is truly a virtue, but even more than that, patience might be pondered as an essential foundation to a host of other desired virtues, including courage, self control, humility, tolerance, generosity, and mercy. Yet the key elements of those most revered spiritual principles remain hope, faith, and love. We can learn a lot about genuine courage and patience by reading Janet's story, coming in this next part of the book.

PART 1

JANET'S GRIM EARLY QUESTS

NEITHER VICTIMS, NOR FOOLS, NOT EVER.

Having been married to Janet these past 27 years, I write as one having unique vision and authority within these stories, which it turns out are too difficult for her to write, especially to complete into any finished publication. I am altogether honored and grateful for this responsibility, as some of these most difficult things need to be told, someway, somehow. For instance, my comments on describing a particularly unspeakable event included later in this section are sadly:

> *"What kind of parent deliberately frightens and then beats a child, less than 4-years old, with a man's belt, especially so soon after a nearly fatal fever requiring multiple days of intensive-care hospitalization? Many years later, Janet still puzzles and suffers over the many unusually extreme and harsh punishments and negativity her parents somehow kept coming up with, while raising two fragile little daughters already damaged by their parents' own negligence."*

During my three score and seven years of life, I have been privileged to work closely with some incredible women in my family, community service, at church, and in the workplace. But, I know for a fact, that none of them could perform to the overall levels of exertion, execution, and grit, as well as with the organized frugality, artistry, and skills that I have seen my wife, Janet, perform multiple times, despite serious physical and medical complications. And I have heard others testify of similar observations before I ever knew her.

Granted, her greatest "super-functional" feats were usually brief, unpaid, and done meekly behind the scenes, where nobody or very few witnessed them. Nonetheless, her proven ability to patiently and humbly sacrifice at levels that nobody else was willing to go, is a well established fact in my experience, and also for a few others. The following stories will help you understand a little about how she developed such an intense drive, and an ironic aptitude to deliver so far above most others' abilities or expectations.

While some have seen and subtly proclaimed or implied her a willing "victim" of her own struggles for various popular reasons, she has repeatedly sought much higher hopes and faith. And she has valiantly and steadfastly held to such fundamental principles, refusing to fully yield to those who snobbishly shame or label such faith as foolish, or sometimes even fanatical.

Thus, she is surely a walking, talking miracle woman to me, and sometimes seems to have unseen angels uplifting and helping her because of her now highly tested faith, and even as a little child. In fact, I believe she must have developed and brought such faith and inspiration as a spirit before she was ever born here. But, don't take my word alone. Please ponder these ironic layers and stories, and decide for yourselves.

One reason I think Janet's story is so important and compelling to the entire subject of this book is because of the unusually vivid and illustrative examples of stark injustice (and related shaming) it presents for everyone across so many long years and situations. Most of those close to us have had no idea that her underdog story could possibly go back that far, and with that kind of terrible injustice and injuries, because it was powerfully hidden, denied, and gaslighted.

As for Janet and me, we wouldn't change anything. Somehow, we are better, stronger, smarter, and happier because of the struggles. Don't forget to look for the tender angels, mercies, and miracles, and the quiet and meek, but sure perspectives and witnesses of a loving and merciful God.

"Patience is bitter, but its fruit is sweet."

—Jean-Jacques Rousseau

"With love and patience, nothing is impossible."

—Daisaku Ikeda

"Beware the fury of a patient man."

—John Dryden

CHAPTER 2
UNUSUALLY HARSH CHILDHOOD ZINGERS

JANET'S MOM WAS THE 'QUEEN-BEE' OF VERBAL 'ZINGERS'.

Janet's mom died eight years ago. Her dad (age 91) currently lives in an apartment attached to our home, and has for the past three and a half years. He now has severe dementia, but very clearly prefers to avoid the care home.

Janet is the oldest of two daughters born to Don and Vera (full-names excluded to protect the innocent). Don grew up on a small marginal farm in northern Indiana. He married Vera and worked several years at a Creamery business, while Janet and her sister, Lynn were born. They then moved the family to the Indianapolis area so Don could take an entry-level job as a fingerprint specialist with the Indiana State Police. Vera would soon work there too, at food-company Stokely-Van Camp's corporate office in downtown Indianapolis.

Vera also grew up on a small farm, about 25 miles from Don. Vera somehow gained a razor sharp, sarcastic sense of humor and wit there, and she developed excellent secretarial and bookkeeping skills. Thus, she always found and maintained full time employment throughout the girls entire childhood and schooling. For unknown reasons, she always seemed somewhat of a "ball-buster", seeking to out-do everybody, even the boys at smoking, swearing, working, and the like.

I don't want to try to cover every detail here, or to fully explain the vast negativity, or even the less frequent positives, within any of it.

However, it is essential that I cover some of this as best I can, if you are to ever understand the rest of this book, and Janet, or even me.

For our entire marriage, Janet has lived with serious health issues, including chronic pain. It is crucial that I have learned from many experiences, whenever Janet cuts me with a harsh verbal "zinger" (though never profane), she is most certainly in real physical pain. In fact, I have learned that those are times that she is probably having a flare-up of her greatest pains, struggling to control it, and to block it out. So, I've learned the hard way to shut up and patiently bite my tongue until it passes. Kindness is free, always kill'em with kindness.

Most of this story has never been fully heard or understood, even by our closest friends, relatives, or even Janet's precious daughters and grandchildren. So it is altogether fitting that it be briefly told now. My intent is to find important positive conclusions by the end of the book, so please bear with me through these painful early stories.

Both Janet and her sister, Lynn, were born with serious congenital birth malformations. Vera smoked three packs a day through Janet's entire childhood, and for many years, Janet had suspected that her mother must have also smoked during each pregnancy.

Vera died eight years ago from esophageal cancer, and Janet never dared to confront her, or even gently ask about the smoking during pregnancy issues. However, several times since then it was brought up to Don, and each time he confirmed it with, "Yes, Vera smoked during her pregnancies, but she never inhaled." As this story fills in, you will repeatedly hear of Don never failing to make excuses to defend and back her up, no matter how wrong she might have been (and vice versa).

Anyway, several others have since confirmed it, but also noted that Vera was prideful and aggressively defensive about baby Lynn's crossed eyes (surgically corrected about age 7), and early childhood asthma (constantly aggravated by Vera's heavy smoking). So, like Janet, almost nobody ever dared mention it, as Vera was never a person anybody ever wanted to agitate, or get on the wrong side of (especially when backed by her big, six-foot-three, stern state police husband). Besides, so many other people also smoked inside the offices Vera worked in during those years, that the 2nd-hand smoke might have contributed as much as her intentionally smoking to satisfy her own selfish habit.

Confirming evidence of all of Janet's malformations did not occur until many years later. However, Janet did have several serious fevers due to urinary tract infections (UTIs) between the ages of two and three years-old and then had to be hospitalized at age three.

Children ages two to three do not commonly get serious UTIs into their kidneys unless there is a malformation of the ureters to the kidneys. Even then in the 1950's, there was a well known surgical procedure to correct this fairly known malformation. But, for unknown reasons, Don and Vera chose not to get that surgery done for Janet, or even mention that it had been recommended.

Thus, Janet continued to suffer chronic and damaging UTIs, having over 100 serious infections during the next thirty three years until this problem was finally surgically corrected at age thirty seven. By then, she was literally allergic or unresponsive to almost every prescription antibiotic known to man, at the time.

THE PERSONAL STORIES, FROM JANET'S OWN FEELINGS AND PERSPECTIVES.

I've known all along that Janet has many more personal details behind each one of these events than what I have been able to chronicle here. Please realize that you will need to hear these stories from her directly (see Appendix: Janet's Own Words), before you can begin to fully understand this book. In fact, she scolded me about "missing the real story" of these UTIs.

Janet's own words and perspectives give many different layers, flavors and feelings that I am simply not able to fully provide here. And, because she is so well-read (has a bachelor's in English) and experienced in Literature and Composition, she seems to expect me to write as some brilliant combination of Shakespeare & Dickens, Steinbeck or Stephen King. But, "That ain't gonna happen. Sorry 'bout dat'." Nevertheless, I've gotten us this far, so please bear with me as I give it my best shot.

Janet remembers being almost 4-years old, riding in the back seat of the car, with Vera driving, and 5-week old baby Lynn lying in the front seat, next to her mom. Don was already at the little house in the

Indianapolis suburb of Carmel that he had purchased for them (with the help of some backing from Vera's parents). Vera was finally coming from northern Indiana with the girls and as many belongings as she could bring. When they arrived, the neighbor lady came over to meet them, and exclaimed, "Why, this child is burning up with fever!" after seeing Janet riding alone in the back seat.

Little Janet had been sick almost constantly over the past year with repeated UTIs, which were treated by a country doctor in northern Indiana. Janet was very young, less than two years old, when these UTIs started, and she vaguely remembers seeing that doctor many times. She was too young to understand most of what was going on. But, she has since been able to piece together that he first treated her with penicillin until she had a serious anaphylaxis reaction. He then treated her with sulfa-drugs, until she had subsequent rejection-reactions to those alternative antibiotics.

Back to the fever; so the neighbor lady ran to her house, called her pediatrician, who subsequently rushed to his car and over to their house. By then Janet's temp was 107 °F. The pediatrician insisted they take Janet to the hospital, where they quickly treated her with a brand new nitrofurantoin drug called Furadantin. The lead doctor told Don and Vera that it was a very new drug that they hadn't used much. He also cautioned them that if it didn't work a miracle soon, in Janet's case, that she would surely die, possibly in the next few minutes, because they had no other antibiotics or treatment options left to use.

Thankfully, the new drug worked. Janet survived that night, and then stayed a few more days there. It must have been a Catholic hospital, because Janet remembers the nurses swishing around in long stiff gowns, and with impressive winged hats that reminded her a little of the bats flitting around the night sky at grandpa's farm. It must have been intensive care because the young child in the bed next to Janet tragically died so very close to her the next day.

Janet remembers feeling afraid and lonely. The visiting policies were very restrictive in 1956, only allowing parents an hour or so each evening. Janet remembers a nurse-nun asking if she wanted a popsicle and wanting to say yes, but she was too afraid to accept such a desired gift from such a strange and unknown person.

One day the nurse brought her into a strange room with huge lights overlooking a cold steel table. They put little Janet on the table and started prepping for something. Janet was sure it wasn't anything she wanted to be part of, so she quickly rolled herself and climbed off. She was almost to the door when the nurse caught her and put her back on, only to have her squirm away again and try to run. The doctor then confronted her and said, "Listen here little lady. If you don't hold still we will have to put those straps on you." pointing to a bigger table with big steel stirrups. So, Janet consented, they gave her an "ether" and completed the procedure.

Janet soon got to return to her new home and family. But, she remembers frequent doctor visits after that, where the urologists would insert painful steel instruments into her little "pee pee". She also remembers her urethra feeling bruised and sore like that after that scary hospital stay-over and procedure, and so she was able to deduce years later that they must have done a "retrograde pyelogram," injecting dye into her bladder to check for urinary reflux, which would explain how Janet's urinary tract kept re-infecting itself into her bladder and kidneys due to a structural abnormality (which was already known to be correlated with mother's smoking during pregnancy).

She remembers her parents complaining bitterly about the costs of that expensive new drug and that she took it every day for over a year, before those urology doctors were satisfied that all of that infection had finally cleared her entire urinary tract.

Janet now sees those remarkable events as divinely guided miracles that saved her life. But she still wonders why her parents could never seem to see or value the heroic people and actions that miraculously saved their precious daughter's life in that way.

Janet recalls Vera, and others, so often reacting minimally to these UTIs as, "just a common bladder infection" until they personally had just one UTI get a little bit out of control, before they could get to their physician for a prescription of antibiotics. Suddenly, they might find surprising respect for anyone who could have possibly endured dozens of them. (If Janet wasn't so ashamed by such frequent and abnormal sickness, and reluctant to even try to mention or explain it to anyone).

In Janet's actual case, over 100 serious UTIs occurred before the corrective surgery (finally at age thirty seven) and dozens more since then, because of the irreparable damage suffered as such a young child.

> Note: If 100 UTIs seems impossibly high to you, remember that Janet has had this serious chronic condition her entire lifetime, and could easily have died several times from it. She is so wary of it, she personally checks her urine every day, and has had to become incredibly adept at feeling, smelling, and seeing any hint of cloudiness in her urine, such that she is almost always correct about when and how she ever got any of these many UTIs.

Also, remember that those early urologists kept inserting instruments into her bladder during that year-long recovery and during multiple other recoveries. So, even if their hands and instruments were always sterile (they obviously weren't), what is the chance they did not drag bacteria into her bladder? I think we should probably not try to question or challenge her personal history estimates on these UTIs. Apparently, those treating her as an adult assumed that she had already knowingly refused the corrective surgery, because none of them ever mentioned it.

About that same time, Janet remembers one particularly nice day at their new home, soon after coming home from that hospital episode. She had just discovered that her shoes made a "crunching" sound in the gravel at the edge of their quiet little street, which sounded a little like the horses in the cowboy shows.

She had been warned about the cars and forbidden to go into the street, but she was only on the edge so she felt okay. She remembers happily pretending she was a cowboy, when Don called her back to the house. When she obediently came, he was hiding behind the door with his belt ready to beat her. She paused as she walked through the door wondering where he went; when he suddenly jumped out, startling her, and proceeded to beat her with his belt. Was this for disobeying, or maybe for causing him to pay such high medical bills? We may never know.

Again: "What kind of parent deliberately startles and then beats a child, less than four years old, with a man's belt, especially so soon after a nearly fatal fever requiring multiple days of intensive-care hospitalization?

To this day, Janet still puzzles and suffers over the many unusually extreme and harsh punishments and negativity her parents somehow kept coming up with, while raising two fragile little daughters already damaged by their parents' own negligence." But, let's go back again, and try hearing and understanding some more about Janet's incredible story.

SYRINGOMYELIA WITH A CHIARI-1&2 MALFORMATION.

After finally getting this corrective UTI-surgery as an adult, Janet's right arm just quit working about a year later, accompanied by searing pain. The neurosurgeon did a quick exam and diagnosed a ruptured seventh cervical disc, but also scheduled an MRI exam to prepare for the coming surgery. The MRI showed a Syringomyelia with a Chiari-1&2 Malformation, which is another serious congenital birth malformation, and a very big surprise to the neurosurgeon.

The Chiari-1&2 malformation means that since Janet's birth, the normal structure that allows spinal-fluid to equalize between the spinal cord and the brain was completely closed (which also causes hydrocephalus, scoliosis, and spina bifida). Over time, in Janet's case, this had caused a huge 14 inch fluid filled syrinx (also called a spinal-tumor) from her brain down through her spine, which by now had crushed the main nerve root to her right arm, and also ruptured the seventh cervical disc. This malformation is also correctable with surgery, but now would require fusing five cervical discs together and cutting through the base of the skull and placing an artificial shunt between the brain and the spinal cord. Of course, the five fused cervical vertebrae would forever prevent her turning her head and neck in any normal way, and that crushed nerve root would now create chronic pain in that right arm… (*Quoth the Raven… …*"Evermore"*).

*paraphrased from Edgar Allan Poe's *The Raven*, 1845. Of course the Raven began quoting "Nevermore" in this beloved classic poem. But the poet later uses "Evermore" for contrast and special-effect.*

"Congenital? There's that word again!"

Don and Vera had come to Minnesota several times to watch their two granddaughters during these surgeries and recoveries. Consequently, they met several surgeons, who were more than a little perturbed at meeting the parents who had contributed to such congenital defects in Janet, and then somehow never had them corrected in childhood, when such defects could have -- and should have -- been more easily corrected, and with far less pain, suffering, and permanent damage to Janet.

I don't know for sure exactly what was said to them, but when they had her sister Lynn on the phone and were discussing Janet's surgery, Vera responded, "Congenital? There's that goddamned word again. My whole life, I keep hearing that word. Dammit to hell, I don't want to ever hear you or anybody else use that weak-assed word again." It helped Janet and Lynn remember a line they had heard so often as kids, "You worthless little wimps. You somehow 'thought' yourself into these weak-assed complaints, so now you can just 'by God' think yourself back out of them."

It also helped Janet remember what Vera had said when she heard that Janet was scheduled for the UTI corrective surgery. She vehemently insisted, "Oh, believe me; You do NOT need that kind of frivolous goddamned surgery."

Janet had let that comment pass as just another complaint. But, as she later thought back, she realized that Vera was commenting as if she knew all along about this corrective surgery's availability, and intentionally kept it hidden from Janet all these years, through all those dangerous UTIs, just to cover her own denial and negligence so many years before. Again, Janet just quietly kept this shocking realization to herself, like all the other terrible things that happened through those years before she met me.

PROFANITY (AND CUTTING SARCASM) BECAME OUR 'NATIVE TONGUE'.

Janet and Lynn both developed unusually strong and gifted talents for hearing and using profanity in sharp, funny and sarcastic ways. Kind of how actor Samuel L. Jackson's affinity for using the "F-word" traces to his abundant childhood exposure.

Janet and Lynn never dared speak that way as children. Although Lynn enlisted in the Army soon after high school and quickly found she could very easily and competently "swear like a soldier". She later married a Navy-man, so she eventually learned to speak it like sailors do, also.

And, though Don and Vera did not apparently use the F-word nearly as much as Sam Jackson, they obviously applied a wide variety of profanity in very colorful ways, always mixed in with copious amounts of mocking, anger, intimidation, and sarcasm.

In fact, Janet is always surprised when so many are so shocked by just the profanity alone, or just the verbal anger. To her, as a small child, she was always primarily concerned and focused on avoiding the threats (and the follow-through) of the physical punishment. This included frequent and unexpected hits to the back of the head and neck (by Mom), or the much harder hits to the lower back, buttocks, and legs with the heavy leather razor strap (usually by Dad). Even their dachshund, Doc, would scurry as fast as his little legs and toenails could go on the slick linoleum whenever Don or Vera got close to where that razor strap hung, because he also got beat with it so regularly and mercilessly.

The little dachshund, Doc, snarled back several times at those beatings (both of himself, and also of the girls). But, each time he was then beaten even more ferociously, so he wisely quit. The girls noticed though, and they both hugged and loved him more significantly than ever because of it.

> ***Please excuse my including these tidbits of profanity in telling these stories. Profanity and abuse are never okay, and certainly not to young children (or dogs). Although, sometimes, such as in Charles Dickens' and Mark Twain's 19th century classics, we really do need to hear the cruel, coarse characters and situations behind them.***

"GOOD BABYSITTERS ARE HARD TO FIND."

Janet was also always very focused on protecting her sister Lynn (four years her younger). After moving south to the Indianapolis suburb of Carmel, IN, the girls were again placed daily into the hands of daycare mother's homes. Janet was soon in grade school, so she wasn't exposed nearly as many hours as Lynn was (except during summers, when school was out).

So, when little Janet arrived after school each day finding baby Lynn needing solace, she formed a strong lifelong habit of providing the best surrogate mothering that she could possibly provide. Often she found baby Lynn sitting alone in an unheated porch with her coat and hat on (wheezing from her asthma in the cold) trying to play with a couple of spare toys. Of course when Vera or Don arrived, the two girls were always both inside the warm happy-looking daycare home.

Lynn's entire early childhood could be summed-up as "failure to thrive". Because she always had to struggle to breathe, she was usually hunched forward, in that asthmatic posture, and always had somewhat sallow-colored skin. These were characteristic traits that would then follow her the rest of her life. She was hospitalized for treatment several times in oxygen tents, and was found with an enlarged heart at six years old. She died last year at 63, due to complications from lifelong asthma, enlarged heart, and brain cancer.

LOOK HOMEWARD, ANGEL.

When Janet was eleven, both girls began going straight home from school and Janet was in charge for a while before their parents came home. Invariably, Janet would be blamed and hit for imperfections or negligence in some of the many daily chores established, especially during summers, when school was out. This included house cleaning, beds, dishes, ash-trays, garbage, lawn mowing, laundry, ironing, and supper preparations. Nevertheless, they were glad not to go to daycare, and both Janet and Lynn very fondly remember those precious times alone, and together.

However, Vera became more blaming, often raging bitterly negative complaints to the girls about her struggles as the years went by. "You girls are as worthless as tits on a nun *(or balls on a priest),*" "If we didn't have you girls, we'd be goddamned millionaires," and, "What kind of damned wimps did I raise, anyway?"

Since Vera was an only child, she knew her parents' small farm would eventually come to her. In fact, her parents contracted with her and Don that if they would start making installment payments, they would not only get the entire farm, but every dollar that they had ever paid into it.

Vera's parents were savers and lived very frugally as their parents and grand-parents before them had. Thus, it was a very sweet deal to contemplate, but unexpected medical costs due to the congenital defects mentioned earlier continued to crop up. They tried to delay the recommended corrections, and hoped their girls might grow out of them, or that they might just go away, but they never did. Instead the medical bills always seemed to get worse, never better. They did manage to surgically correct Lynn's crossed-eyes, only after waiting until her 1st grade school failings were obvious.

Don always really loved money, savings, investments, and fancy new 'drop top' convertible cars. Janet remembers him having seven different convertibles. He told me about another he had when he first met and courted Vera, in the late 1940s.

Thus, he was totally supportive of the plans and payments to get the farm, and after exactly twenty years of service in the state police, he was able to fully retire, at age 45, so they sold their house in Carmel, and moved up to the farm. By then, Vera's mother had died unexpectedly at age sixty three, both Janet and Lynn had graduated high school, and Vera's dad had remarried and built a small house in a nearby town.

"ZINGERS" CUT BOTH WAYS (FOR GOOD AND FOR EVIL).

Vera had a charismatic and narcissistic power and pushy-ness in her personality, and she also knew how to use her sharp tongue to be funny and fun with her sarcasms and wit. Vera's parents were good, generous, hard-working people who were beloved by most everybody in their area. When Vera's mother died, the funeral and wake were overflowing, and both the funeral home and the church could barely fit all of the large bouquets of flowers.

Whenever they had visited back home, during those Carmel years, both she and Don carefully presented their best and happiest (and their humblest) foot forward, at least by appearance. In fact, shortly after moving back to the farm, Don ran for elected office to the County Board of Trustees, and won a surprise four-year term, despite running as the minor-party underdog against the heavily favored dominant party incumbent from their township. Vera even got paid as his Township Secretary, part-time.

But, why was Vera so bitter, harsh, and profanely negative towards her own young daughters? And, why did Don back her up so loyally and unfailingly? Although Vera was clearly the dominant mind and voice behind most of the harsh words (the Queen-bee), both daughters confirmed to me that they overwhelmingly feared and hated their father more (he was bigger, angrier, scarier, and he *always* hit harder). At least Vera contributed plenty of twisted but humorous anecdotes embedded into her harsh sarcastic insults, which helped Janet and Lynn to secretly laugh or quietly giggle together through so many of those hardest times.

In the 45 years since Don's retirement from the state police, he has clearly shown a strong aversion to any kind of physical work. Maybe that's why he loves investments, money, and rare coins so much; because he could always use them as excuses for so much time spent sitting and studying them. Vera, on the other hand, worked past Don's retirement and was always much more active in involving them in climbing the status ladder outside their immediate circle. In fact, she miraculously and discretely manipulated Don's application and door to door campaign for Township Trustee, with just enough time before the election to not cause too much concern to the favored incumbent opposition.

Vera was also a terrible complainer. Always taking offense, or justifying a reason to be offended (and angry) especially towards Janet, Lynn, and other vulnerable scapegoats around them, blaming, shaming and complaining to them for any and all of her troubles, including Don's "lack of action." I suppose their vulnerability made them so much less able to dare to mock her back, or call her out (to her face, anyway) for such pathetic whining or complaining. Don didn't complain as much, but "Nobody ever gave me anything," was his favorite complaint, and is still heard plenty of times by anyone around him now.

Somehow, Vera and Don seemed to gleefully enjoy it together when they found almost any type of mistakes in others. Either to mock, rage, or scoff at, or if found in their own daughters, to often give harsh, intimidating, and physical punishment (as if the personal value of the punishing discipline justified the harshness, so they were actually snobbishly doing you a favor in their minds). Some might say they were a bit addicted to the exaggerated mocking and rage (as some sort of "rage-a-holic" partnership).

For example, Janet remembers one of her very worst beatings, being a severe belt strapping by her dad (about a supposed F in English, which has always been Janet's forte), but it being directed by her mom, who insisted that Janet be completely naked in front of her "stark raging" father for its full effect. Janet was in eighth grade, about fourteen years old, and only another woman, especially a mother, could possibly know the fullness of that shame for a girl of that age. But, obviously that was Vera's objective in directing it that way.

The next day at school, Janet's closest girlfriend stepped up and helped make the excuses for Janet to skip gym class. She wanted so much to help the terrible situation, but she knew well from previous "strappings" how ashamed and fearful Janet was that if the school (or anybody else) ever called her parents about any bruises or strap-marks, that poor young Janet would surely be punished even more severely.

Don and Vera always seemed attracted to remembering, and mocking the worst about anybody, but almost never the best. When Janet was about ten, she left her little purse at a road-side cafe. She got the purse back, but for some twisted reason she never heard the end of it from her parents. They used that small mistake of an innocent ten year old to label and mock her as unforgivably and ridiculously "forgetful" her entire life.

The shame from their pushy and endless, merciless mocking of this innocent mistake eventually disturbed Janet so much that she started feeling brief panic attacks whenever they would mention it. Several times as an adult, she fearfully found herself having unusual and serious subconscious spells of forgetful short-term memory-loss while in their presence. And, even in middle age, she had to occasionally leave for a while during visits from them, to stave off what felt like some sort of seriously possible nervous breakdown coming on.

When she finally more fully described it to me, I insisted we break off visits until she could decompress those crushing stresses; which resulted in about fourteen years of "heaven sent" distance and needed relief for Janet's poor strained and frazzled nerves.

Although Vera always loved to dangle and manipulate with monetary-promises and threats, carefully but snobbishly leveraging her inheritance prospects over their poor daughters, or other ordinary less-fortunate people around them. Don was usually the "hard guy" to voice and enforce the actual blame and excuses for always reneging on any promised (dangled or implied) financial supports for Janet's or Lynn's college, loans, weddings, cars, travel costs, support for grandchildren, family heirlooms, or any chance for family inheritance. He always cited vague 'tax penalties' into his long lists of blaming excuses.

I guess nobody can ever understand any of it completely. None of the family and friends from back home ever knew much about how their daily lives really went down in the big city (and none of them had any comparable farm inheritance coming, which allowed Don and Vera to retire at 45 with a unique power and status over so many others). As I described above, whenever they had visited back home, during those Carmel years, both Vera and Don hypocritically faked their very best, happiest, and humblest faces forward.

Later, during their retirement years, Don and Vera burned through many sets of "best friends". For odd unexplained reasons, they could always seem to find ways to attract such so-called best friends, but could never seem to keep them very long. Janet was always sure that these friendship troubles held clues to understanding the toxic personality aspects of her parents a little better.

Before Vera's dad died, they strategically refrained from any new or convertible "drop-top" cars, and lived carefully and frugally on the farm as he and grandma always had. When Vera's dad finally died, he left her the farm and all of his savings and possessions as promised, so they were quickly able to go back to Cadillacs and convertibles. However, he had much later and near his death added several stipulations that would eventually eat up a significant amount. Requiring a generous gift to one close nephew of his, and $15,000 each year to his widowed 2nd wife, as well as free habitation of his home in town for the duration of her life. These all sound reasonable, but she (the 2nd wife) proceeded to live another thirty-three years, which caused great grudging resentments and some seriously difficult depletions to Vera's beloved inheritance.

WHEN THINGS REALLY GOT A BIT MORE TENSE.

Vera was attractive and always had a very nice variety of popular designer clothes, shoes, and matching purses for her office work (like a true Queen-bee). Janet and Lynn were both very young, but Janet remembers Vera having long, flirty, whispery telephone conversations with someone, during a period when Don was enrolled in college extension classes, after work and on weekends. Vera would often leave Janet with toddler Lynn alone in the car for several hours, while she went into a mall during this period. She always got very dressed up, including carefully placed makeup and perfume, for these extra long mall-visits.

During a weekend visit alone with Vera's mother, little Janet (about 6 years old) somehow sobbingly described enough of such recent behaviors that both her grandparents questioned her at length to learn as much as they possibly could about that. Janet then remembers Vera coming back to the farm and becoming unusually submissive and tearful to both her grandparents, and to Don. Thus, things got a bit more tense back home in Carmel, Indiana.

TO ANY LOUD "DAMMIT!", WE ALWAYS ASSUMED THEY WERE ONCE AGAIN BLAMING "JANET!"

Janet, of course, was far too young back then to fully understand her parents, or their abusive dysfunction, and when parents are shameless, children always bear the shame (or at least come running or do anything to try to make things better). Vera and Don would never admit to any personal mistakes or weakness, so they would always complain, blame, or shame someone else for any inadequacies they felt, or saw in themselves.

Even now, over 60 years later, Janet has great difficulty trying to understand it herself, let alone describing or helping someone else to understand it. It's taken me 27 years, and she still doubts my full understanding of her stories, or my ability to write this.

In fact, she wonders now how she ever survived those years. But, she simply had to survive for Lynn's sake. Luckily, the abundant love from tender loving grandparents (only about 100 miles away) helped enormously.

Janet vividly remembers events around the unexpected death of her maternal grandmother. She was 17, a senior in high school. She was called out of class to the principal's office. There she was told that her parents would be picking her up, because someone in the family had died.

Even though she would soon be off to college at Ball State University with multiple opportunities to leave this abuse and dysfunction behind, losing that grandmother at that time plunged her into such a dark hole of loss and grief that Janet started seriously thinking a lot about personal suicide.

Janet remembers not fearing the death part in the least. But, she was very afraid of failing, and then she realized the clinching argument again. She just could not ever leave Lynn alone with such abusive parents who had proven to care so little about her beloved little sister.

> *Note: If you, or anyone you know, are feeling like Janet was at this time (now or ever); Please, speak up and ask for help. And please don't quit. Please keep going. Just a little farther. Just a little longer. There's always help up ahead. You can get to it. You will never regret trying a little longer. Besides, you can't just leave your loved ones behind like that.*

Ironically, it was always quite clear that Don and Vera considered Janet their favored child, which was a scary thing for Janet to contemplate (given her lifelong worries about Lynn). They often complained to Janet that she was an 'under-achiever'. But, Lynn was repeatedly labeled a *worthless* "throw away," which was even more appalling and unacceptable to Janet.

By Janet's senior year, things had gotten as bad as they would ever be, physically and emotionally. Despite the handle literally falling off that old razor-strap from so much abuse, Janet now had absolutely no hope that anyone from outside would ever notice or be able to stop it. After all, Don was now a high ranking, highly respected law enforcement officer with the state police (he was now Chief Fingerprint Expert, testifying in major court cases), and her closest, most trusted grandparent was now dead and gone.

The same grandma who had amazingly noticed something, and questioned six year old Janet enough to confront Vera. But, unfortunately she and Grandpa had totally focused on the marriage problems, when Janet was desperately hoping they would hear her tell them about the unnecessary and hurtful *hitting*, which was already seriously disturbing and damaging little Janet, and her beloved little sister, because it always intensified and made the constant verbal threats and other mental and emotional abuse so much worse to contemplate.

Janet remembers being afraid to tell anyone about the hitting. So, she remembers thinking, "Maybe I should start by telling Grandma about being left alone in the car. Then I can slip in the hitting later." But again, her grandparents became so focused on Vera's marriage behaviors, the hitting once again never got any serious attention.

Years later, Janet discovered a calendar she kept during her senior year. It showed lots of babysitting for neighboring families. And, it showed a small X for every day her parents hit her (which was still almost every day). Even though she was by then a very capable and responsible young woman, soon to be off on her own, they were still irrationally beating her, as if she were still an irresponsible and belligerent much younger child.

One irony of parental abuse like this is that at least Janet and Lynn had parents very intensively and physically present during their entire childhood. In fact, in so many ordinary families today, parents run or hide from their parental responsibilities (in many diverse ways). And, sometimes that shirking of parental responsibility and presence can be more damaging to needy children than what Don and Vera did to Janet. Vera did expect an awful lot from Janet, and she was abusively harsh. But, she also spent time carefully showing and teaching Janet valuable skills and examples that would actually bless her many times throughout her life.

After all, despite her many medical defects, and serious surgeries, Janet has proved many times during her life, an incredible ability to be *"super-functional"*. She completed her degree at Ball State U in 3-years (including summers), worked at the federal building in downtown Indianapolis, and then landed a high-school teaching job (of only 2-English spots in the entire state at that time), despite there being an over abundance of teachers at that time. And even now, as an aged grandma, I think she is surprisingly proving to be the humble but heroic underdog champion within all of these long hidden and long-suffering struggles. Thus, the hurts and damages so easily remained hidden by Janet's normal functionality.

Lynn enlisted in the Army, as soon as she could without a parent's permission. She must have discussed the risks with the recruiter, because when she came home and informed them, Vera immediately grabbed her and started slapping. But, Lynn raised her fist and commanded her to stop, "I am now property of the U.S. Army, and I *will* have you arrested if you ever harm me again." Janet was newly married and living in Pittsburgh, and she could hardly believe it when Lynn told her. Yet, she felt overjoyed that her vulnerable little sister now had the moxy to actually stand up to them like that. (To this very day, Janet has never presented such an argumentative stance in their presence or within her letters, like Lynn courageously displayed several times over.)

Thousands of times over the years, Janet has felt fearful enough of others' outside disapproval or judgments that she was severely reluctant to go out in public. Similarly, she often felt like compulsively curling up in a dark-corner and hiding from the entire outside world until the blaming and shaming feelings and dialogues could somehow subside a bit in her mind. But, she has only actually physically allowed herself that kind of obsessive compulsive cowering a few dozen times in her entire life.

Each time it happened, she would surprise even herself, and eventually find a way to feel and hear her 'still small' inner voice** and to pick herself up, and get back to her work. But, ever finding someone (besides Lynn) who could tangibly listen carefully enough, or long enough to understand even a small portion of the most terrible parts of this story, now that always seemed somewhat impossible for her to hope for.

Please ponder the quiet spiritual power and 'light' provided here to this abused and vulnerable child/adult; and quietly search within your heart to feel and find that same inner source of comforting peace and genuine courage to pick yourself up and move forward again. Janet and I both believe that this 'still small' inner voice is a key answer to the imminent question: "How did Janet survive this dark* *treatment so much, for so long?" This book will revisit and explore this aspect of quiet spiritual power and 'light' built deep within each of us, in several later chapters.

Even now with me writing these details, she has serious doubts and fears that these stories won't be fully accepted or understood by most people, or even read at all, because her parents so successfully suppressed them to everyone around her, her entire life (see: gaslighting), until I came along. (Note: of course, besides carefully hiding and tailoring the truth for others, Vera and Don always found subtle ways to make sure it was always very clear to the girls who the outside world would believe, if they ever tried to tell or make a case against them, in any way, to anyone.)

Janet has always had to struggle with some repressed anger and the verbal "zingers" she learned, by violent subjection from her parents. She made -- and mostly kept -- a strict vow to never hit her own daughters (even though those two tall, strong, athletic daughters have infrequently rebelled, and emotionally blackmailed and attacked her, both directly, indirectly, and passive aggressively).

Janet's response to such rebellions has almost always been to step back, to remember her childhood, and to mildly defer to patience, kindness, and gentleness. She very carefully controls her anger and her tongue around most people. Once in a great while, especially when in great pain, Janet will lose control of her tongue in her struggle for control of the chronic pain, but she always regrets it, and usually quickly reassures with some sort of gentle kindness.

Even to her parents, she has always shown quiet, if not sincere, respect. She has also made huge strides in forgiving them (of course, with help from many prayers, and much divine Grace), while carefully never forgetting any of it.

The only person to which I've ever seen Janet really let go of any of her core reservoirs of repressed anger is me. Believe me it hurts, because she has lots stored there, and she is good at venting it. But to anyone who might feel afraid or intimidated by her, don't be. If she ever did unload on you (she won't) she would surely quickly follow up with kindness, gentleness, and love unfeigned. I alone can attest to that.

Janet has a powerful unique gift for appreciation and admiration of great literature, art, performance, and especially music. I love music too, but I am repeatedly in awe of her sense for the hidden and embedded power that some uplifting music can have for touching, enriching, and even saving us from our sufferings and sorrows.

Janet also has an incredible gift of putting on a happy face and attitude, no matter how sick, or pained, or low she might be feeling. A close friend observed this enough times that she titled it "The Janet Jones School of Acting" and referred to it many times before I ever knew Janet. I can testify of the incredible power of this gift to effectively fool almost everybody around Janet, even me. Janet developed the gift out of sheer survival (and apparently shame, that unless she appeared almost perfect, nobody would ever accept her as normal).

Janet's oldest daughter developed the gift in abundance from watching her mother display it so often. I think she thought her mom was doing it simply to please others. I'm pretty sure she and the friend who labeled it had no idea how deeply ingrained into Janet's psyche of survival and self acceptance those gifts, masks, and skills go for Janet.

INDISPUTABLE MEDICAL PROOF

Many years later, the surgeon correcting the kidney malformation had repeatedly asked her a series of questions, "When have you had serious blunt force trauma to your kidneys? A car accident or fall; maybe a mugging?" "No." Janet had heard these same questions asked by so many different urologists during those many years of repeated UTIs, that she had concluded that these questions must be standard to all urology exams.

But this time, Mayo Clinic's Head of Urology intervened, and asked; "But, have you ever had blood in your urine?"

Janet's mind had to flounder through many memories before she was able to flash back to several of the worst back-strappings by her father, where she did have seriously bruised welts higher on her back and blood traces in her urine for days afterward. But, before then, she had never imagined it might have damaged her kidneys. "Oh," she finally realized, "That's why they had always kept asking about falls or muggings."

Then, less than a year later, the neurosurgeon correcting the spinal malformation asked her about the whiplash damage showing in her neck in MRI scans, "Have you had any repeated whiplash, maybe from several serious car accidents?" This time Janet's mind more quickly flashed back to the frequent and unexpected hits to the back of her head and neck whenever her mother felt rage about some complaint or another.

For example, because Vera was such an excellent typist (repeatedly able to test well over 90 words/min with zero mistakes), she drilled Janet for weeks. Sure that if she drove her hard enough, Janet could at least perform somewhere close to her typing skills.

But, Janet's spine and arm were already damaged enough (by the yet unknown and hidden syrinx spinal tumor) that she would never be able to come close to Vera's typing skills. Janet remembers working extremely hard, but plateauing below the minimum expected 40 words/min level, and her mom unexpectedly whip snapping her skull and neck so hard by hitting her with the heel of Vera's hand that her forehead flew forward and nearly dented the typewriter multiple times, and that Janet's neck was then tender and sore for weeks after that.

Janet also remembered seeing Lynn wince and shrug so often after Janet got hit in the back of the head and neck, because Lynn knew the same was coming her way. Janet seldom had a chance to wince or shrug, because Vera was so good at ambushing her first, before she knew exactly when it was coming.

> Surgeon: "Did you ever feel or hear the back of your skull cracking, followed by hissing and the salty smell/ taste of spinal fluid?"
>
> Janet: "Yes, I had that many times, but I never knew that was important or unique."
>
> Surgeon: "What about headaches? You must have had terrible headaches."
>
> Janet: "Yes, I did, but Mom always threatened and mocked me if I complained, so I learned to never mention them."

Surgeon: "I just can't understand why your parents didn't have those checked? The syrinx would have been detected, and much more readily corrected back then."

Later, during the recovery from the brain surgery, the neurosurgeon got remarkably serious with Janet, "You very clearly have the highest tolerance for pain and abuse of any patient our team has ever seen. In fact, we all feel a strong need to caution you to be careful that you do not mentally block out your various pains so much that such pain blocking might somehow kill you." And, then she added, "We have documented the physical damage to you as apparently due to negligent/ abusive parenting, in case you ever find a need for such documentation or legal recourse. It's now here in this sealed envelope in your file."

Wow, thought Janet. She had always thought nobody would ever notice, let alone advocate on her behalf. "Maybe somebody truly is finally looking out for me for a change."

DAMAGED CHOICES

Just after these surgeries, Janet's 1st marriage of 17-years had become stressed to the breaking point. Thus, her husband John (full name excluded) had moved out, and he was living in an apartment close by. The pending divorce was merely lacking final approvals. Janet had tried everything to keep that marriage together, but a combination of her past plus some extra fatal input (to be explained a bit later into a subsequent chapter) from her parents had seemed to doom it from the very start.

John's odd insecurities made their match work well, at first. His odd need to constantly belittle her (which traced to their earliest courtship) felt very 'familiar' to Janet, and connected with her twisted 'family-fantasy' that such belittling treatment was really just some kind of convoluted love. And, of course John never had, and never would, ever hit her, so that actually seemed like such an enormous, unbeatable improvement to her unsuspectedly damaged psyche.

Looking back, Janet now clearly realizes how much her (and Lynn's) damaged psyches contributed to her poor choice of John as her spouse as well as to many other vulnerable and poor choices they both would eventually make.

Janet lost one child, due to miscarriage. And, during both successful pregnancies (requiring C-section surgeries) her body abnormally retained fluids, because of the UTI damages, dangerously gaining well over 90 pounds, and causing scarring and adhesions that would eventually become serious problems.

Such pregnancy difficulties did also serve to reveal (and slowly help convince Janet) more about John being an exceptionally poor match for her lifetime of underdog struggles. His incessant needling followed by, "What's the matter? Can't take a joke?" which Janet always took as innocent intent and never objected to, clearly evolved into snobbishly cruel taunting, and much too hurtful to bear at the very end.

Both her parents and John often vigorously criticized and mocked Janet for not pursuing a career to increase their family income and status. There was just nothing Janet could ever say or do to get them to ever let up on that subject, so she never really tried defending her position. Nevertheless, given her background with daycare, she was ready to stand against their cheap mocking forever before she would ever give in to send her daughters to daycare.

Note: Neither Janet or I want to discourage the use of daycare, or criticize the quality of most daycare providers. In fact, we have both provided and used daycare many times in raising our own children, and helping with our grandkids. We both believe the quality and options have greatly improved since the 1950s-early 60s when Janet's worst experiences occurred.

Janet's obstetrician and his colleagues strongly cautioned her about the serious risks of proceeding with both of her successful pregnancies. John never came to any of those consults or check-ups. When Janet explained the risky drug treatment, and months of mandatory bed-rest to help prevent another miscarriage, John surprised her both times strongly insisting that he preferred to not have any children, especially any damaged or disabled child. Even though he consistently proved that by how little help or attention he ever gave to childcare, Janet never quit hoping for a change in John's attitudes on children, which were so hard for her to understand or accept.

WILLING VICTIMS OR FOOLS? NO, NOT EVER!

We will eventually see how Janet's vulnerabilities will increasingly go sour against her (Chapters 6, 7 & 8). But, the inevitable labels or the blaming and shaming accusations that she intentionally or selfishly chose to be the "victim" or the "fool" in these stories to get sympathy or attention is exceedingly cruel, unfair, and *untrue* (see Part 5, Chapter 12). In fact, although those cruel and false labels have haunted her since early childhood, I am quite sure that you will never find anyone who has proven more times, and with more effort, and more overall sacrifice, that she does not deserve those labels, and has never nonchalantly allowed those cruel accusations to be so easily used against her, either fairly, or unfairly, ever again.

"Out of the night that covers me
Black as the pit from pole to pole,
I thank whatever gods may be
For my unconquerable soul.
In the fell clutch of circumstance,
I have not winced nor cried aloud.
Under the bludgeonings of chance
My head is bloody, but unbowed.
Beyond this place of wrath and tears
Looms but the Horror of the shade,
And yet the menace of the years
Finds, and shall find, me unafraid.
It matters not how strait the gate,
How charged with punishments the scroll,
I am the master of my fate:
I am the captain of my soul."

—Poem by William Ernest Henley,
now entitled "Invictus" 1875.

You will eventually see throughout this book that Janet and I are clearly what some would call an "odd couple" in many odd ways (an odd understatement). Although we were both repeatedly smeared with implied blame and veiled shame as the ironic victims and fools of our own struggles, those implications were never accurate, for many reasons. Thus, we are neither willing victims, nor fools; in our innocent lifelong quests to find genuine unity to help rescue our beloved American Dreams, which is a good subject and theme for this book. Because *"Struggles make us stronger, so the BEST is yet to be."*

No one is ever really an "island", entirely isolated by themselves - alone. Everyone is connected and a part of this beloved and universal "American Dream" and human family. If anybody's hopes or best ideals get bullied, diluted, or washed away, we are all diminished. Because we all need each other's best hopes and best ideals, more than we are yet able to understand. So, as you read our stories and quests, please be patient about how they might help inspire and relate to you. Patiently ponder these things yourselves and do not doubt your best faith, or fear the mockers so quickly or easily, for all of these stories and ideas are specially put here, for each of you.

We will eventually revisit how Janet's personal story goes even more sour, in Chapters 6, 7 & 8, but somehow she never gives up, never becomes bitter or selfishly offended, and we don't regret any of it. So later let's see how such abuses and "zingers" might relate to greater issues found infecting the broader world around us.

"That which does not kill us makes us stronger."

—Friedrich Nietzsche

RISK BENEFITS, TENDER MERCIES, AND BLESSINGS.

I asked Janet why she thought God had let so much adversity fall on her and Lynn. She said near the end of her marriage she prayed and even screamed at God, reminding Him of the many great promises in the scriptures. Finally, after hours of ranting and sobbing off and on for several weeks, a profoundly peaceful feeling came, and she prayed that she was willing to take any suffering if it would soften John's heart. Then only a few weeks went by before she was scheduled for the second UTI corrective surgery to her bladder and kidneys (the 1st corrective surgery failed five months earlier, thus had to be repeated).

Janet got a priesthood blessing at that time that said, "You will experience no pain. And, if you do feel pain you should remind Heavenly Father of this blessing, and insist that He honor it." And then he said, "Your husband and you will then grow together, first spiritually, then mentally, and finally physically." The man voicing the blessing was not a physician or a marriage expert. He was the husband of a friend who loved Janet very much, so Janet thought to herself, "He has no idea what he is saying and must want very much for me to have that blessing." But she knew the pain part would be completely and utterly impossible.

Janet had already endured the pain-filled recoveries from two C-section births and one other major abdominal surgery, and each of them involved excruciatingly painful recoveries. (Note: This other major abdominal surgery was actually the duplicate UTI correction, because due to some twisted whim of fate, the first surgery failed and had to be repeated.)

But, the Mayo Clinic anesthesiologist visited her before the surgery and said, "When children get this same corrective bladder surgery, we always give them a spinal-epidural for the first day of recovery. Would you like to get that?"

"Oh, yes, I've been dreading the pain so much."

So, he agreed that is what they would do. And so, when Janet woke up from the surgery, she was very surprised to feel no pain.

Of course, she was numb and paralyzed from her toes to her shoulders from the epidural. When the anesthesiology team came to visit her the next day, they said, "Let's roll her over and inspect the epidural needle and for the prospect of bed sores." But, Janet had a hanging-handle within reach, and said, "I think I am strong enough to pull up and angle myself." So she did. Thus, the surprised team let the epidural needle stay in that day. Each succeeding day she expected them to pull the epidural needle, but each day they came in and decided to let it stay in another day.

Janet's urine bag started out black with blood, and stayed that way for four days, which was over three days longer than they wanted, so the healing recovery was taking much longer than expected. Because of Janet's many UTIs, C-sections, and previous failed corrective abdominal surgery, she had unusually large and problematic internal scarring adhesions, which had required the surgeons to cut her wide open from hip to hip, and much extra cutting to deal with the many internal adhesions. And, because the first bladder corrective surgery failed, her poor scarred-up bladder now had been cut into pieces a second time and stitched together a second time. But, this time she remained numb with surprisingly little pain.

Janet began to remember the words of the blessing, and that she had thought those words completely impossible, especially since she was still recovering from the pains from the failed surgery, only five months earlier. Now, she was miraculously feeling almost no pain. In fact she remained totally numb where the healing was occurring. And, it was taking significantly longer than normal. Her urine bag was now cherry red colored, and the anesthesiology team kept coming and leaving the needle in another day, each time. One of the assistants was surprised, saying he has never seen them leave the needle in for more than two days.

Eventually, the epidural needle was left in for seven consecutive days, and the urine bag now had turned pink and finally even yellow colored. Besides healing the hip to hip cuts through multiple layers of scarring and abdominal muscles, you might be able to imagine how much your bladder might hurt from that much surgery, realizing that the painful sting of salty urine would be constantly present while that much healing was occurring within her bladder.

To correct the malformation and to stop the urinary-reflux backwards to the kidneys, the uretures had to be repeatedly woven through the muscled-layers of the bladder's walls. And, to do that they had to completely cut the bladder apart, and then sew it back together again.

So, Janet began feeling more and more blessed by this. She then started remembering and puzzling over the rest of the blessing. "Your husband and you will then grow together, first spiritually, then mentally, and finally physically." That wording seemed immensely perplexing to Janet, because of all the many aspects of healthy relations that she and John lacked throughout their entire marriage, a healthy physical relationship was not one of them. They had never had problems with that part of their marriage. Nevertheless, she felt so blessed about the pain promise that she decided to have complete faith about the husband part, too.

John was now getting more and more uncomfortable and surly, even telling Janet several times how old and ugly she looked, and that he wished she would just die so he didn't have to divorce her. Then, less than a year after the bladder-kidney corrective surgery, she got another blessing (from the same man that had given her the earlier blessing), which included the words, "...something is about to be revealed that will require all of your strength and faith to overcome." Some friends wondered if it might be the impending divorce, but Janet, feeling a 'still small' spiritual whisper in her heart and mind, said, "No, it's another health problem of some kind." Soon after that, her arm stopped working, and the defect causing the fourteen inch spinal tumor, which had been there since her birth, was revealed after being hidden for so long.

After the two major brain and spine surgeries and recoveries, Janet finally agreed with John to sign the divorce papers. John hated that these terrible surgeries and hospital recoveries had accumulated hundreds of thousands of dollars in medical charges, though they were mostly covered, but more embarrassingly revealed some of his serious selfishness and failings as a husband. And, so they first separated during the UTI-surgeries, then went ahead with the finalizing of divorce papers after the final spine surgery.

Then, I came along about two years after that, as an extremely vulnerable and emotional wreck, and Janet was soon to be again reminded of the strangely worded blessing, "Your husband and you will then grow together, first spiritually, then mentally, and finally physically."

I said earlier that we are an *"odd couple"* in many different ways, and during this time period particularly, we were both very surprised by the incredible strangeness of events occurring. It was as if God was almost pushing us towards each other spiritually and mentally for some unknown reason that we both felt quite surprised and more than a bit uncomfortable about, because He was also testing us physically and emotionally.

For a while, we both fought against the idea or possibility of us being friends in different ways and for different reasons. Nonetheless, God seemed to know better, and found divinely creative ways to put us in each other's pathways and parties. I guess He knew that we would eventually become a very formidable *"odd couple"*, strong enough, and patient enough to tell and promote better understandings of these important stories and issues.

Janet, of course, knew that I mostly needed spiritual and mental encouragement after the endless and impossible negative reactions by my wife, friends, and family. And, of course she and I both knew the terrible risks and perils of any hint of romance or physical attraction to each other. But, she also recognized better than anybody else around me how deeply and seriously hurt, damaged, and vulnerable I was, and for some reason she was willing to risk it and/or even suffer it for my sake.

I remember her taking enormous time and effort to try to give me a different view of myself than the ones I had been getting back from my wife and family for so long. When I objected, and refused to accept her new reflections, she merely found other wisdom and evidence until she finally began to turn my poor and almost destroyed self images around.

CHAPTER 3

UNDERSTANDING JANET'S PARENTS.

Janet estimates that I have only mentioned a 100th part of the total harsh details that could be told here. You might argue that at least Don and Vera never *sexually* abused Janet or Lynn, and that would be true. But, sending the girls to many different daycare homes over eleven long years eventually even provided that missing item on the abuse checklist. Janet, understandably, does not desire to subject you or herself to any more of those sexual details or issues than she has to, so it won't be detailed further. But, Don and Vera both confirmed it in response to moving letters that Janet wrote to them, many years later.

Janet never did anything with the medical documentation for legal recourse mentioned earlier. She did however complete a wide variety of personal counseling and talk therapies. She sent several loving and heartfelt letters well before her mother died eight years ago. They were rejected with angry replies. Interestingly, they did not deny anything. In fact, Janet was very surprised that their replies actually affirmed most of what she wrote about, including their deep knowledge and mishandling of the serious child sex abuse, mentioned briefly earlier since "good baby sitters are hard to find". Yes, besides the hospital file of documented parental abuse, Janet now also has received written letters affirming many of the most damaging childhood abuses, in their own handwriting.

Janet still loves her parents, and knows that she always will. Don and Vera both came from lovely families, and as far as we can tell, all lovely people and lineages. Janet's love and forgiveness for her parents is understandably complicated by some serious unresolved distrust and even some lingering repressed anger issues. Whatever she has been able to forgive is surely helped by God. She has tried hard to understand them and any possible psychopathology they might have suffered or inherited. She realizes that any second hand psychoanalysis probably does not have much value, but will offer some generalities later as examples for this book, or for future discussions with anybody who is interested in that sort of thing.

One interesting irony/perspective is that Janet's childhood has remarkably negative elements of abuse that compare and even in some respects exceed those of the worst serial killers, and other seriously broken or psychopathic people. Yet, she somehow took a pathway to greater goodness, sacrifice, service, and understanding for others. Try to explain that?

Psychotherapists seem to always need more examples of both the victims, and also the perpetrators of such extreme abuse. Pertaining to Don and Vera's unique and collaborative abusive examples, and the many ways they encouraged and backed each other up, they need to be understood, avoided, and prevented at all costs. This doesn't pertain just to abusive parenting, but also the entire family and community dynamics that allow and even encourage gang bullying among those most vulnerable within their ranks. We as Christ followers are commanded to forgive, but never to forget. Kindness is free, always kill'em with kindness.

One aged and experienced counselor asked Janet, "Why aren't you more broken? I've had thousands of patients and clients sit here with me, so broken and dysfunctional from abuse, that they will never be normal functioning. And yet, the abuse they told me about doesn't even begin to compare to yours. I am trained and experienced enough to know that you are not exaggerating. You are minimizing, and I know you have not told me everything. In fact, you are by far one of the most abused patients in multiple ways that I have ever professionally counseled. So, what is your secret? Why did you survive, without being more mentally or emotionally broken than you are? Please tell me so I can use it to help others."

Of course, Janet did not have any complete answer for him. I'm not sure we can answer all the questions about these things, even now. We will, however, try to answer as many as we can. Earlier, we provided the following side note: (We submit it again, now, as the best short answer we can give. Of course, fulfilling and serving her role in the family, with sister Lynn and Grandma and Grandpa, helped enormously also.)

> *"Please ponder the quiet spiritual power and 'light' provided here to this abused and vulnerable child/adult; and quietly search within your heart to feel and find that same inner source of comforting peace and genuine courage to pick yourself up and move forward again. Janet and I both believe that this 'still small' inner voice is a key answer to the imminent question: How did Janet survive so much, for so long? This book will revisit and explore this aspect of quiet spiritual power and 'light' within each of us, in several later chapters."*

Carefully telling and writing this story has been a very long, hard effort, but also very therapeutic and valuable to Janet and to me. We know that many who eventually need to know about this, and deserve to know about this, may never actually read it. But, at least Janet knows that she did her part to bring these things into the light, and we are trying the best we can. Everyone, please write or record your stories. The rest of us really do need to know them.

Again, Lynn died last year at age sixty-three due to complications from asthma, an enlarged heart, and brain cancer. And because she was Janet's only co-witness to many of these things, Janet felt even more of a need to get them recorded now, somehow. Thank you all, for helping us get some of this heard and understood better.

Since our marriage, Janet has more recently been able to compare many notes about her parents, with Don's younger sister (Auntie Marilyn) and Vera's step-mother (Evelyn). As it turns out, each of them had quietly endured many years and episodes of mistreatment from Don and Vera, but each had always been very afraid to share such information with anybody else (fearing the same kind of repeated intimidations and wrath from Don and Vera that they had already suffered previously).

During several trips through Indiana I was able to meet them and listen as they very guardedly compared such notes with Janet. Each was exceedingly pleased to finally find someone willing to hear their side in these matters, likewise very surprised and shocked to hear even some of the whole child-abuse story from Janet's and Lynn's perspectives.

Again, these different family members helped provide another set of important perspectives for me to gain a better overall understanding of these matters. And, helped confirm to me that these stories absolutely needed to be told and written or recorded in some way.

Janet has no desire (or knowledge and ability) to judge the overall intentions or reasons behind her parents' actions. Nor does she want to hurt or to denigrate them. I guess the fact that she has waited until her mom has been dead for over eight years, and her dad is ninety one and of a seriously failing mind, says something about that. We believe that these stories will help add examples and understanding for the rest of this book. And, we hope they also help someone out there who may have experienced some challenges or struggles related to abuse or "zingers" like them.

GRATITUDE AND RESPECT FOR THE "DIVINE ROLE" OF MOTHERHOOD.

Quickly blaming parents rather than carefully understanding and honoring their work and sacrifices seems to be a common modern mistake these days. Janet's example encourages everyone to be more careful about making those mistakes.

Janet didn't get to have a wonderful stay-at-home mother. But, maybe that's why she appreciates great mothers so much when she sees one. And, despite Vera's faults, Janet never complained to her, and even now prefers to remember the few good things over any negatives.

Per Truman Capote's interviews, even the most murderous convicts fondly reminisce to their prison-mates of even their faintest sweet-memories of good mothers. And, obviously they never take kindly to modern-misfits who so quickly disrespect their own good mothers, which so many convicted felons are not lucky enough to have had.

Janet always says that the best response to negative criticisms and reactions is to just have the very best and happiest life that you can possibly have, given your circumstances, and to doubt your doubts before doubting your faith. So, this book is our answer to that wise perspective. We *do not* regret any of it, because all of it has helped us to become stronger, and better people, than we would have or could have been, had we had things come more easily for us. We have truly tested our faith and beliefs ourselves over a very long run of popular opposition, and proven the adage of "struggles make us stronger, so *the best is yet to be.*"

COPING SKILLS AND STRATEGIES.

Janet and Lynn were very young when these harsh childhood stresses started crushing their feelings, and literally their physical health and wellbeing. They both, at times, withdrew into maladaptive mental escapes of denial and fantasy-daydreaming. In fact, Lynn's emotional fantasies and overeating for comfort became problems which seriously cursed her adult life.

I described how Janet's fantasies about suicide were helped and stopped by her habitual caring and worrying for her sister, and the "still small inner voice" that she had learned to quietly listen for and to trust. Somehow, these extra burdens of responsibility, care for Lynn and for her parents' harsh demands kept little Janet from slipping further into any maladaptive behaviors.

I believe they actually kept Janet trying different things, until she began stumbling across more healthy and functional approaches that I can recognize in her, even today. For instance:

- Her ability to bravely admit and face fears, mistakes, limitations.
- To embrace vulnerabilities, and keep trying something else that might work.
- To find solace in humor, laughing, music, great stories, and literature (especially the scriptures).
- To keep pondering and praying and learning about the root causes, and to find genuine gratitude wherever possible.
- To believe and act as if true-change and repentance is possible.
- To patiently serve others, even when they don't acknowledge or appreciate it.
- To quietly, patiently, and courageously sacrifice, or even suffer for the sake of others.
- Kindness is free, always kill'em with kindness.

(HOW) TO KILL A MOCKINGBIRD?

It is significant that after Janet's divorce, she needed employment to support herself and her two daughters. Her teaching certifications had lapsed, but she found temporary employment on several big educational testing projects as a reader of essay responses to generic literacy prompts, such as, "Describe your favorite childhood toy." She eventually became a leader and trainer; helping groups of readers validate and standardize their scoring of such responses. Deciphering these responses was difficult in southern children taught to read and spell phonetically, especially when they added extra syllables to capture the various southern accents and drawls (For example: flips was repeatedly written by one boy as "fleops")

Again, *"Janet never dreamed back then that she would ever be inspired or find a connection to a real future book title. But, in one of the states, the students had studied Harper Lee's "To Kill a Mockingbird" that year, and so were prompted to respond to that book. Many of the responses were quite surprising (and funny), including those who incorrectly remembered the title as: "HOW to kill a Mockingbird", and even, "The Killer Mockingbird".*

And again, I can testify that this book and title are no coincidence. Many heroes, angels, miracles, and tender mercies have come forth to bring it to pass. It has brought us hidden treasures of peace and comfort, to both mind and soul, And, it can bring the same to you and yours, if you give it half a chance.

PART 2

MY QUESTS

FIXING "GENUINE COURAGE AND UNITY"

WORDS MATTER, AND VERBAL "ZINGERS" MATTER MORE, ESPECIALLY AT THIS "ALARMING APEX" WITHIN THE INFORMATION AGE.

"Zingers" cut both ways (for good and for evil) and they reveal important hidden truths about any and all leaders and social movements using them. Today they are revealing an escalating war of extreme "Us vs. Them" opinions, theories, and rhetoric that some say is already growing into a second U.S. Civil War. Words matter, and I personally refuse to sit back and quietly allow this alarming "Apex" of exaggerated "Us vs. Them" polarization to so simply and easily divide, corrupt, and possibly wreck our peace, our faith, our hopes, and even our beloved American Dreams.

Those fundamental American ideals of freedom, fairness and independent self-reliance, self-respect and responsibility, along with plenty of individual opportunity for wholesome pursuits of happiness, have continuously attracted and united the best people, minorities, immigrants, and refugees from almost every nation and era. I still positively and patiently plead along with Abraham Lincoln, *"that this nation, under God, shall have a new birth of freedom—and that government of the people, by the people, for the people, shall not perish from the earth."*

—Gettysburgh address, 1863.

In fact, this book presents stories, experiences, examples and ideas supporting the positive notion that we can still adjust, repair, and even possibly fix the angry divisiveness, hypocrisy, and corruption mentioned above. We can begin unity, not by censoring "zingers" or extreme opinions, but rather by listening and understanding them better, so that we avoid or prevent them from being used so extensively, and powerfully by elite leaders. These include some modern-globalists or socialists and other ambitious populist-snobs intent on using them to divide us for their own selfish political, economic, status, or celebrity gains, making victims and fools of us all. Thus selfishly creating large (but foolishly fickle) popular "bandwagons" piled high unto themselves.

I believe that, if we can also begin to inclusively and respectfully gather the very best and most positive ideas from everybody (even those pushy populist-snobs), and patiently put them together towards the development and promotion of a sort of peaceable and respectful theory, or story, of everything, or in other words an inclusive and genuinely unifying "Epic of Evolution," then I believe that we can use those positive ideas to build and repair many roads and bridges between us. (More explanation on this "Epic of Evolution" term coming in Chapter 5.)

Please excuse my liberal use of the derogatory labels "snobs", "victims", and "fools". Such labeling is never okay, and certainly not when identifying specific people. I am intentionally risking using them here, to demonstrate (from both Janet and I) our intense and knowledgeable awareness of the victim blaming and shaming we have struggled against, and our awareness of why and where it comes from. I submit, because of my frequent references to "zingers", and our unique personal struggles with this subject, that I need some leeway to adequately demonstrate and fully address these issues.

*** "Suckers" and "Losers" would also fit nicely into the above footnote as the events and examples unfolded within the banner years of 2020-21. The U.S. Capitol Building became an ugly and murderous crime-scene, when citizens angry about lost elections, recounts, and challenges smashed and defaced its marbled sanctuaries during important congressional sessions to officially act upon the election's electoral results. Five people died and many serious injuries resulted, 138 police were injured, and the sanctity and security of our beloved Capitol Building will never be quite the same again.***

CHAPTER 4

THE IRONY OF VERBAL ZINGERS.

The year 2020 is breaking norms for verbal zingers pertaining to pandemics (such as Covid-19), as well as presidential impeachments, tweetings, and election campaign chaos. Next, a "2020 Twilight Zone" of endless Covid precautions, shut downs, canceled events, and social distancing started, with no sure end in sight.

Then, angry riots, looting, and burnings cropped up over unfair treatment against vulnerable underdog minorities, including big government mandates, profiling, and police brutality, even starting in my own beloved homeland, notorious and known for pleasant and harmonious "Minnesota-nice" sociality. Whatever lessons we are learning throughout this banner year, I think they will not be soon forgotten.

Why verbal zingers? Good question. I, personally, am probably more surprised at this word choice and subject area than any of you are. But, words matter, and people's safety and dignity matter most of all. Nevertheless, other than the events and times of 2020 mentioned above, you'll just have to read further to get the full answer.

Note: I do hereby apologize for my repeated usages of the word **zinger**. I love words, but no word should be overused, and I know that I am treading perilously close to crossing that line with this mostly uncommon and funny sounding word.

For your information, my wife, Janet (to whom this book is dedicated, and whose story is so prominent herein), doesn't *love* my choice and use of this sparsely used word; she actually hates it. But, I now believe we will all begin to see that "zingers" is a good choice within this book, as we dig deeper into the next several chapters. **What exactly are verbal zingers?** They cover a wide range. **Are zingers always a bad thing?** No, but most do tend towards the negative and hurtful. Some have studied them and referred to them as "loaded language," similar to propaganda.

Again, *words matter.* Words begin to matter even more as they are crafted together to reveal the ideas, and the *intent* of those ideas. The entire history of mankind is filled with rich recorded evidence of important and competing words, *ideas*, and ideologies.

The prominent leaders (of both thoughts and actions) within this competing "War of Ideas" have often used zingers to help make their messages more effective and powerful, and to attract and grow numbers and support from followers. This book explores the who, what, when, where, and hows of such zingers. And, more importantly, it explores the various ironies and the hidden aspects that they reveal about those who use them extensively.

THE BEST AND THE WORST WAYS TO GET SOCIAL CHANGE.

The best leaders (and zingers) for change have always insisted on responsible, respectful non-violence, both in words and actions (and in ethics and morals), no matter how much harder, or longer it takes. Such leaders usually *patiently* try to go as positive as possible, with any negativity quickly and carefully followed up by some kind of respectful and gentle reassurance.

For some examples, think of Martin Luther King Jr., Dalai Lama, Mother Theresa, Nelson Mandela, and Mohandas Gandhi in recent years; and of Jesus Christ, His key Apostles, their many martyred followers, and other prophets from more ancient times. Let's call these best leader types "servant leaders", or "servant personalities".

In contrast, the most selfish and corrupt leaders (and zingers) have always sought the quickest, easiest, and most popular pathways possible to success and social change (in words, tone, and in actions) no matter how indulgent or disrespectful, divisive and extreme (they almost always use the age-old "***the end justifies the means***" rationale someway, somehow).

And, sometimes (more covertly) use the situational ethics of "***almost anything is okay, as long as you don't get caught***".

Let's call these worst leader types "authoritarian leaders", or "authoritarian personalities", who happen to trend toward the most selfish, snobbish, or unethical end of the curve. It's sad how common these kinds of leaders (and zingers) have become, and how increasingly common they are becoming in almost every field and profession.

Another common aspect of these authoritarian personalities is how quickly they complain and blame someone else to cover for their own failings and to sort of capitalize on the build-up of negativity. And, how smart and skilled they are about carefully choosing and shaming their carefully selected and vulnerable "scapegoats".

Janet's parents were ordinary, everyday examples of such expert scapegoating, even using their own daughters, and other vulnerable people in their own families and community. (Remember such expertise from Hitler and other fascist, pushy populist cults of personality, as clear examples on the much bigger national and world stages.)

One huge irony in the current situation is that any of us, even as reluctant followers of those selfish and corrupt leaders, need to also share in this responsibility. Many of us have begun to lose our sense of individual and collective responsibility and respect for each other and ourselves. Because everyone loses big chunks of self-respect and responsibility, as soon as we allow ourselves to be led down these quick, easy, popular pathways to change, we start approving and supporting such snobbish materialistic success and status, or even merely start pretending, denying, or looking the other way.

Especially those groups led by the ambitious and pushy populist snobs, intent on using zingers to shame, trivialize, or divide us (or their scapegoats, but actually making victims of us all) for their own selfish and corrupt political, economic, celebrity, or status gains, despite simultaneously diluting down everybody's moral and ethical standards.

Shame on any of us (or all of us) who just sit back and allow this to happen, especially to our children, or to our weakest and most vulnerable underdog minorities (often unfairly blaming them for being the willing victims or fools of their own struggles). This kind of common and populist 'victim shaming' is hugely hypocritical and abusive, and needs to be monitored, and much more effectively discouraged or prevented.

Of course, we can't always directly choose all leaders or policies. And, it often seems that we have no choice or agency in the important situations and events of our lives. Well, that's exactly what they want you to think, so don't allow it. "Act, or be acted upon". But, be patient, and never expect genuine change to be quick or easy. Kindness is free, always kill'em with kindness.

WHY 'THIS APEX OF THE INFORMATION AGE'?

I love the recent explosions of information access and technologies that have played such a critical role in advances in every field of prosperity, and of knowledge and studies. I also love that so many of the inventors and leaders of these technologies have been born and bred right here in the good old U.S.A. I believe it is no coincidence that the U.S. clearly set the modern example and standard for the most free and open societies and nations of today, and that it has done so through a singular national constitution that many of its leading authors and founders very sincerely witnessed and testified was 'divinely inspired'.

Despite this alarming 2020 Apex of angry disharmony, I really hope and believe that these recent explosions of info access will provide us important opportunities to adjust, repair, and even possibly fix the angry divisiveness, hypocrisy, and corruption mentioned above. After all, terrible crises have so often brought out the best in America, and all of us as Americans.

I mentioned "elite modern globalists" and "ambitious populist snobs" above, as if I intended to name them. I will not name anybody in a negative sense (other than the Hitler examples), but I will detail my thinking on such. For now, please understand that I support global trade, competition, economics, and diplomacy. I have nothing against ambition or populism in general. I also accept that some things are best done by governments or can *only* be done by governments.

However, I do object to those who shamelessly promote big global programs, military, agencies, corporations, and governance as the only modern and reasonable solution to every problem, and every feasible future (while subtly diminishing free markets and hiding the truth about how terribly gridlocking, inefficient, ineffective, hypocritical, wasteful and destructive many of these big globally governed programs actually are). I also object to the many pushy populists that unnecessarily use such angry and disrespectful exaggerations and extreme rumors and protests (as well as propaganda) to shame and divide us for their own selfish gain (despite often dangerously diluting down our moral and ethical standards).

Please do not be offended or focus on one or even just a few examples of these leaders or zingers. Surely, some leaders and zingers provide extreme examples, but I sincerely hope we can begin to see these as verbal tendencies creeping into all of us, including the chronic bullying behaviors of our children on our playgrounds and social media platforms.

WHY THE IRONY?

I love that so many aspects of freedom of speech and freedom of religion are again being tested within our U.S. culture and thus within the continuing interpretation of the U.S. Constitution and Bill of Rights. It is very clear (and ironic) to me and many others that we as a people and nation do not fully understand our own First Amendment rights and responsibilities as much as we think we do. That these rights and freedoms are *not* absolute rights, and they do not come without some very messy and complicated limits and responsibilities.

For example, the U.S. Supreme Court opinions about freedom of speech clearly have ruled that protests and criticisms against the government are protected far more than criticisms or protests against private individuals or private organizations. The Founding Fathers were especially aware that free expression against powerful governmental heads has always, throughout human history, been the particular speech in dire need of protections. Many powerful empires and rulers throughout history have bragged about their citizens' freedom of speech and religion, but then selectively and hypocritically smashed those most critical to or different than themselves.

Note: More recently, these obnoxious and ubiquitous tendencies to blame and shame carefully selected scapegoats are subtly and hypocritically making victims and fools of us all. See the recent blaming/shaming of low level front line police and journalists for merely conducting difficult, sometimes nearly impossible, task assignments for the safety and well being of everyone. Also see the incessant accusations of "fake news" towards any and all reports that don't align with a particular populist view, all while those of that populist viewpoint are hypocritically spreading far worse exaggerations, extreme conspiracy theories, and half-truths. And, this isn't new or confined to politics alone. Although the 'fake news' label is new, similar tactics have been used in religious disputes and in other realms, as well.

The establishment clause in the First Amendment forbids government entities to favor one "state religion or church" above others, or to the disadvantage of any other religion, church, or non-religion. Clearly the powerful state churches of Europe had over-bullied their competition to the point where fair minded people could no longer stomach such intimidations and humiliations.

I need to repeat here, *"Most of us see religion or churches as only those who worship divine entities. However, in this increasingly secular and modern, materialistic world of ours, many ordinary citizens today feel strongly that these new secular ideologies and philosophies are quickly becoming the new religious (or non-religious) bullies within our culture. And, thus as the newest and most currently favored "state religion" (and despite their non-religion claim and status) they should be forbidden, or at least limited in how much they can infringe upon -- or bully -- any other church or religion."*

Ironically, I really believe that all these "struggles make us stronger, so the *best* is yet to be". I believe that the rich diversity of irony being created and found within the verbal zingers of these times cuts both ways (for good and for evil) and that they also reveal important hidden truths about any and all social leaders and movements using them, that can help guide us in adjusting, repairing, and even possibly fixing the angry divisiveness, disunity, and problems mentioned above.

"Go ahead and hate your neighbor,
Go ahead and cheat a friend.
Do it in the name of heaven,
You can justify it in the end.
There won't be any trumpets blowing,
Come the judgment day,
On the bloody morning after
One tin soldier rides away."

—Lyrics published in 1969 by
Dennis Lambert and Brian Potter.

DOUBT YOUR DOUBTS, BEFORE DOUBTING YOUR FAITH.

Many years ago, I began compiling and writing some personal story items about my wife, Janet, and me. But, I kept getting stalled over complicated doubts and fears about misunderstandings of some sensitive feelings and perspectives on difficult family issues, including divorce, bigotry, and even shocking levels of abuse. I knew the stories were important, so I kept jotting notes and outlines. But, since Janet is the brilliantly verbal English major, and I am more of a "somewhat serious and quiet, sometimes verbally challenged engineer/scientist", I really thought that I would end up encouraging and assisting Janet in writing some sort of story. Especially one for actual publication.

I believe I did help encourage and prompt Janet to write several important letters to her parents, back then. But she was unable to do much more than that. The stories and the efforts to write about them were just too stressful and hard for her. It's now 2020, I have semi-retired within this last year, and pandemic social distancing is creating more free time for me, and many others.

I actually started getting more serious about publishing something from all of my notes and outlines about five years before my retirement target. I began bouncing ideas and even writing some possible letters and chapters, but as before, I kept getting stalled over complicated doubts and fears. What exactly should I write, and how will I get it published and promoted? I do not want this book to be just about me, or Janet. However, I now feel strongly prompted that our personal stories can provide useful examples for discussing and understanding some much bigger stories and truths.

I highly encourage all to doubt your doubts, before doubting your faith. That includes your considerations of the warnings and extreme examples cited in this book, either specifically or in vague generalizations. The last thing I want to do is to cause anybody else to doubt the best and most positive parts of their traditions and character, as well as their faith in the good, better, and best things around them.

I hope you will forgive me for the many sarcastic and satirical potshots I have included herein. I have tried to generalize them to help us all see that we are all part of the problem, and thus we all must be part of the cure. Kindness is free, always kill'em with kindness.

Janet has several cousins, friends, and their husbands, who enjoy gently posting simplistic puns and "dad-jokes" on social media, hoping for reactions. Janet, having studied English-literature, in turn enjoys gently chiding them about how pathetic such humor is, when compared to the great and witty word-plays found in the greatest literature ever written.

I believe these "pun-posters" enjoy those gently chiding reactions. And, I believe that such gentle humor, satire, and sarcasms can provide wonderful breaks from the serious struggles all around us. I hope we all can find more time and reasons to ponder and share such gentle humor with each other as we seek to sort out our doubts and fears, from our best ideals, and this humble writer's appeal to "the better angels of our natures."

IS A "THEORY OR STORY OF EVERYTHING" EVEN POSSIBLE? COULD IT HELP UNITE US, IN UNDERSTANDING?

Albert Einstein employed powerful theories and thought experiments in his work. Near the end of his life, he was working hard to find a "Theory or Story of Everything", including the elusive elemental forces and matter particles of gravity.

He didn't completely find it, but he sincerely thought that he was close to such a theory, and that such a theory would have power to unite people towards easing and maybe even preventing many of the ideological disagreements causing so many violent protests, world wars, and chaos during his lifetime. Since then, theoretical physicists have managed to establish a growing body of thinking and research around a universal "String Theory", which seems to provide what Einstein was looking for: that "Theory or Story of Everything", including explaining somewhat the elusive forces and matter of gravity.

Incidentally, this universal "String Theory" requires eleven total dimensions (in order for the mathematics to work out correctly). Since our current physical universe only contains three dimensions of space, plus one dimension of time, we can only directly measure a total of four. The seven remaining dimensions required by the math indicates parallel universes, and a possible theoretical foundation for unseen spirit dimensions (which have been sensed and even 'seen' in visions and dreams by so many people, from so many different cultures and times).

The creation/evolution controversy has been raging ever since Darwin's book *On the Origin of Species* in 1859. Over fourty years ago, the phrase "evolutionary epic" was coined, in hopes of improved respect and unity, mostly in the heated science vs. religion debates of those times. Since then, many outstanding leaders have worked towards development and promotion of similar phrased ideas, including the "epic of evolution," which according to *Taylor's Encyclopedia of Religion and Nature*, encompasses the following:

> *"a narrative that blends religious and scientific views of cosmic, biologic, and socio-cultural evolution in a mythological manner. (the 14 billion year narrative of cosmic, planetary, life, and cultural evolution—told in sacred ways. Not only does it bridge mainstream science and a diversity of religious traditions; if skillfully told, it makes the science story memorable and deeply meaningful, while enriching one's religious faith or secular outlook.)"*

I believe that especially at this "Alarming Apex" of the Information Age, when all past recorded information is so readily available to each of us, that a universal "Theory, or Story, of Everything" can be successfully developed and patiently progressed upon, and that it can help unite many of us like nothing else in recent times.

I believe that positive change is possible for individuals and for nations, and that a new birth of freedom is still possible here in the U.S., especially at this time of alarming negativity. The year 2020 is forcing valuable lessons of patience upon us all, whether we like it or not. I hope that such patience will also help us all escape some of the pushy and snobbish populist enticements, and slow the growing influence of many of those greedy leaders. I will explain more about these ideas and give more details in the later chapters of this book.

Albert Schweitzer, highly distinguished winner of the Nobel Peace Prize and holder of four PhD degrees, sought for years for the basis of a new worldview which could help ease some of the angry divisiveness and polarization happening throughout the world. One day, while in a boat on the river in Gabon, it struck him with great force and clarity: "Reverence for life".

> *"Reverence for Life says that the only thing we are really sure of is that we live and want to go on living. This is something that we share with everything else that lives, from elephants to blades of grass—and, of course, every human being. So we are brothers and sisters to all living things, and owe to all of them the same care and respect, that we wish for ourselves."*
>
> —Albert Schweitzer.

CHAPTER 5

IS AMERICA SUDDENLY NOW A DECLINING LOST CAUSE?

OR, IS IT EXCEPTIONAL?

I love America, but it isn't perfect. Not now, and certainly not during its first eighty seven years when it was struggling a lot from the curse and hypocrisy of slavery, and the unjust mistreatment of Blacks, Native Americans, and other unpopular and vulnerable minorities (including some serious women's issues, family, marriage, alcohol abuse, and child safety issues).

From its very beginnings, the U.S. has been at the center of the most tumultuous set of changes and crises that our entire world has ever seen (especially when considering the short 245 year period of its existence). Changes from dramatic religious and political revolutions and reformations in Europe, and several rounds of "enlightenment" and "great-awakenings" here in the Americas. And, continuing crises occurring from the rapid economic, social, cultural, industrial, and colonial changes throughout the world. Driven by new technologies, educational opportunities, and incredible inventions improving transportation, communications, mass media, manufacturing, health, nutrition, and almost any material convenience and entertainment you can think of, these changes and challenges seem to redefine the U.S. in each new decade, and to help many of us to finally begin to discover our overall hopes, faiths, and destinies.

AMERICAN EXCEPTIONALISM

If America is to be considered Exceptional, which is a topic being bounced around a lot lately, such exceptionalism cannot be just because of the typical tangible reasons cited. Neither can it be just because of the abundant and rich land resources, or just because of its hard-working and motivated people, or even just because of the rare combination of freedoms that its Founding Fathers and founding documents established for its heritage.

No, I personally believe that America is exceptional because, besides all those reasons mentioned, it's been blessed (and has been long before its beginning as a nation) by an unseen and mostly indescribable, but undeniable gift and spirit of positive hopes and dreams (perhaps the American Dream?) that has reached out and touched so many people, from so many distant lands, and across so many thousands of years. And, if we dig just a little, we can easily find it here today in abundance.

Martin Luther King Jr. spoke of it in his famous "I have a dream" speech. Long before that, Christopher Columbus witnessed and wrote of it, then risked everything he and his backers could afford on it, through multiple voyages. The many groups of religious pilgrims coming here spoke and wrote volumes about it.

My ancestors saved and planned and then risked everything they had to come here. Wave after wave of immigrants and refugees from almost every land and time have felt its touch. Many for religious reasons, but many others for economic and other reasons.

The ancestors of most of you, and most everybody that I have ever known, had been touched to some degree by this unseen spirit of hopes and dreams about a promised or blessed land called America (even before it was called that). I know that some of you doubt the reality of God or of such a spirit of hope, but I think all of you will have to agree to some degree, that this idea or hope called the American Dream has existed for many people, and still exists and motivates many people today.

In fact, the U.S. Founding Fathers believed that the Bible prophesied of it. And, when George Washington took the oath of office to be the first president, it is recorded that he opened the Bible to the 49th chapter of the book of Genesis *(https://en.wikipedia.org/wiki/George_Washington_Inaugural_Bible) (https://www.youtube.com/watch?v=VOA1oagp1-Y)*, and that he placed his hand specifically at verse 22, the verses where Father Jacob is dying in Egypt, and thus proclaiming his last words of blessings for each of his twelve sons (verses 3-27). Washington was of British descent, and believed that the blood of the lost ten tribes of Israel (headed by Joseph's double portion tribe; see Ephraim & Manasseh) had been scattered northward, and planted in Britain. The special words blessing Joseph's tribe state (with some possible-interpretations and **bold font** added by me for emphasis); verse 22 "Joseph is a fruitful bough (or branch of the family tree), even a fruitful bough by a well (or sea?); whose branches run over the wall (a barrier, like the Atlantic ocean?)"; verse 26 "...unto the utmost bound of the **everlasting hills**..." (to a blessed and promised land, containing an endless chain of mountains -- such as the Rockies and the Andes-- from America's tip to tip?). Comparing the words of Moses (about 500 years later) upon his coming death, similarly blessed each of the twelve tribes of Israel (Deuteronomy 33: 3-27); verse 16 (blessing the tribe of Joseph) "And for the tops of the **ancient mountains**, and for the precious things of the **everlasting hills**". Further comparing Jacob's and Moses' words of blessings provide many intriguing words for thought, and reasons to ponder about all of the tribes of Israel (especially the scattered and lost ten tribes, which are repeatedly prophesied to be "gathered in the last days." That is *all* tribes, not just the tribe of Judah).

AMERICAN DECLINE

Is America (and thus the American Dream) in decline? Yes, I believe that comparatively, America has recently slipped somewhat in comparison to the outputs and other economic measures of China and the combined European Union, Japan, and other rapidly developing Asian countries. I also believe that America has slipped some in other areas of leadership due to a general moral and spiritual decline of its leaders and people (including a general diluting, or 'watering down' of important principles, ethics and morals). But, I believe that America and the American people still possess enough to lead in some areas again, now and far into the future. Especially since America continues to be a gathering place for the brightest and best minds and spirits, who always seem to want to come here, as if they were called by the whisperings of an unseen spirit of hopes and dreams.

For example, throughout its history, America has been able to step up mightily for itself and for others, during times of crises, such as during WWI and WWII, and during many other wars and crises or disasters, whether man made or not. The U.S. has often been able to bring almost miraculous assistance and aid, time after time.

Now, unfortunately we sometimes cannot seem to even adequately keep the peace and security within our own borders. And, as discussed earlier, the exaggerated and extreme polarization between us is causing some to warn and prepare against a second U.S. Civil War. Some top historians are comparing today's disharmony with other great U.S. crises and finding it worse today in significant ways.

But, we're still strong enough to lead in many important areas. Many people resent us showing and using our great military power so often around the world. We should try to be much more careful and wise about that. But, there are many other areas of leadership that the world still desperately needs and wants us to provide a positive impact.

CREATING HUGELY POPULAR NETWORKS OF VICTIMS OR FOOLS.

Is it possible that we have become overly spoiled by our own prosperity, overly comfortable in our leisure and retirement vacations, and overly wanting or expecting everything to be quick, easy, and popularly approved? Can it be so much so, that we are now more susceptible than ever before to almost any type of exaggerated or faked positivity, and to the slick sales and marketing of ambitiously corrupt populist con-men in politics, business, education and schools, churches and religion, sports and entertainment, and especially in any areas of self-help or self improvement?

We all have struggles. And, we all have weaknesses and vanities that can make us vulnerable to incursions from extreme scoundrels, scams, counterfeits, and confidence men. Is it possible that many of our most elite, ambitious, and successful populist U.S. leaders are actually trying and succeeding to attract and create huge networks of victims and fools? These are important questions that need to be explored. Please ponder these from your own personal perspectives.

We all have tendencies and potential to "self sabotage" ourselves or self-destruct by foolishly seeking and choosing the quick, easy, and popular options. Examples of this potential can be found in many of the leaders who have heavily promoted those options. They gained the confidence of the people based upon quick and dramatic popularity and pseudo-success. But, when it became apparent that their promises and success were actually a sham, or a "ponzi scheme" their fall was usually quick and often involved prison time.

Certainly, nobody wants to admit to being made a victim, or fool. Most snobbish populists or peer leaders or even the worst certified bullies or bigots (victim blamers, or shamers) will actually seldom ever use those derogatory terms. But, a quick and easy overview of our most popular national politics, entertainment, protests, advertising, religion, and fringe media makes a huge case for the U.S. allowing ourselves to be made suckers, victims, losers, and fools, whether we are willing to admit it or not.

Of course, our most successful populist leaders are not complaining, because they are -- and have been-- profiting from all of these things for the last several hundred years. In fact, top historians have warned and shown examples of these "power brokers" repeatedly and selfishly re-writing the histories around such issues. I mean many of those most elite, ambitious, and successful U.S. leaders in almost every field, including business, sales & marketing, church & religion, community organizations, sports & entertainment, and government & politics.

Today, the rest of the world is very aware of the incredible wealth, and mass-media domination of the U.S.A., including the Hollywood glamour, the movies, television, reality TV, gossip media, and vast social media. Of course, they love some of it. But unfortunately, much of it leaves them with a declining impression of America, and Americans. They surely know of our many serious hypocrisies and pathetic chronic problems, rampant amongst our average citizenry (including our children) such as seriously increasing:

- Anxiety, depression, and chronic sleep deprivations
- Obesity and other unhealthy eating and fitness disorders
- Bullying, gossip, blaming and shaming victims
- Suicide, rampant divorce, domestic abuse, and mass shootings
    - » Endless child bullyings, suicides, and even human sex trafficking
- Alcohol abuse, and serious illegal drug abuse (even of prescription drugs and medications), addictions and other maladaptive and self-sabotaging behaviors
- Chronic organized crime, and illegal drug and murder networks
- Social protests which quickly resort to looting, burning, and violence
- Chronic Scandals, and scams by ambitious, crafty scoundrels
    - » And somehow respected counterfeits, and confidence men of surprised levels of status (backed by hosts of faked positivity, unity, and legitimacy).

Certainly, we can't always choose our leaders. We are often temporarily stuck with less than the best leaders and policies. Violent demonstrations, tantrums, or even revolutions aren't the answer, either. Very often we must patiently do our parts the best we can, and merely seek the best genuine unity that we can find. We can always work, vote, and use our personal choices and pocket books to "Act, and not be acted upon".

IN SUMMARY: EVERYBODY MATTERS; ESPECIALLY THE UNDERDOGS.

I sincerely believe that there is only one race; the Human Race, or the human family. We all matter. Everyone is precious and important.

We all struggle, but nobody's struggles are exactly the same (or perfectly fair, by any worldly standard). We all have feelings and opinions and faith, but nobody's feelings and opinions and faith are exactly the same, or more important than anyone else's.

It was not fair for Janet and Lynn to be born with such congenital malformations, and then further subjected to such blaming and shaming abuse. You will later see that their lives will continue to be cursed by blaming and shaming, even accusing and labeling them victims and fools of their own struggles. But, they both tried harder and more meekly because of those unfair injustices.

The greatness and beauty of nature and of creation lie in the marvelous diversity and individuality of every life and every soul. And so, the diversity of our individual struggles, feelings, opinions, and faith should be celebrated, and should unite us in positive peace, hope, faith, and love, that we all might be supported and included, and that nobody's feelings, opinions, or faith should ever be trampled, or excluded. Because if somebody's feelings, opinions, or faith gets trampled today, then anybody's or everybody's feelings, opinions, or faith might be trampled tomorrow.

I believe that we should never ask, require, or force people to dilute their fundamental faith, ideals, hopes & dreams, or morals & ethics, just for the sake of some quick, easy, or modern ideology or alliances. Rather, I believe that we should encourage everyone to constantly search, find, and hold fast to the strongest fundamental ideals that they can possibly find for themselves and for their posterity.

Again, I believe that most people yearn for some kind of improved unity. Not any two-faced, faked or forced unity or positivity, but a much more genuine, respectful, and lasting unity in our homes, marriages, families, communities, schools, and churches.

- Words matter
- Underdogs matter
- *All* struggles matter (especially and ironically, those of any long suffering vulnerable underdogs) or even metaphorical *"mockingbirds"*.
- Change matters
- Genuine unity matters

All ideas and zingers for change matter, especially by any leaders with enough heroic Patience to establish, preserve, and/or repair some level of genuine unity vs. faked unity back into our precious "American Dreams").

In fact, I still believe with all my heart and soul that our blessed American Dream, together with the American ideals and the U.S. Constitution, still holds the keys to achieving this lasting *genuine* unity.

It's never too late to change, or to choose more hope and truth in your life. It's never a mistake to make the better decision, no matter how unpopular or mocked the choice. Hard work eventually **–trumps--** talent and riches, every time.

> *"The way to get started is to quit talking and begin doing."*
>
> —Walt Disney

> *"Make no little plans; they have no magic to stir men's blood and probably themselves will not be realized. Make big plans; aim high in hope and work, remembering that a noble, logical diagram once recorded will never die, but long after we are gone be a living thing, asserting itself with ever-growing insistency."*
>
> —Daniel Burnham.

But, after reading all of this; How do we 'kill' the Mocking Birds? Kindness is free, always kill'em with kindness.

PART 3

OUR COMBINED QUESTS AND STORIES

OUR LIFE TOGETHER.

As I said earlier, I do *not* want this book to be just about my wife Janet or me, or focused on any specific or selected populist leaders or users of verbal zingers. I strongly believe that this subject is far too big and important to let it focus on just one or even a few examples. Nevertheless, since I am writing --and narrating-- this journey, I believe you will want and appreciate knowing some aspects from Janet's and my personal stories, which have gotten us to this perspective, and to this point in time.

Janet and I are clearly an *"odd couple"*, in many different and ironic ways. We have many different opinions and views. And, even when we agree, we usually have different approaches to act or react. But, I am increasingly seeing how that actually makes us much stronger and more influential to many others.

I sincerely believe that we would never have found or chosen each other were it not for the many remarkable events, and tender mercies to be revealed in the following stories and pages. I think you will be surprised by some remarkably inspiring patience and courage, but even more so by the long-term underdog aspects. Nobody wants, or ever chooses to be a vulnerable long-term underdog. Or do they? ..."Struggles make us stronger, so the *best* is yet to be".

CHAPTER 6

THE IRONY WITHIN OUR INNOCENT PERSONAL INVESTIGATIONS.

MY SOUL-MATE.

My wife Janet frequently "zings" me with cutting, sarcastic verbal zingers (though never profane), and many of them hurt quite a bit. In fact, she is so talented and practiced at composing and delivering such zingers that I believe that nobody I have ever known could even hold a candle to her, given a contest of such. So, why don't I resent her, and hate her for hurting and cutting me so sarcastically?

1. She has very credible reasons from her past history (covered in Part 1, Chapters 2, 3).
2. She has proven, many times, in many ways, to be the most understanding and loyal person towards me that I have ever found in my entire life. And...
3. I do sometimes fall a bit short in my responsibilities, so then I need (and sort of want) to be reminded, and humbled.
4. She has demonstrated incredible abilities to inspire and encourage other people, even besides me. Proving multiple times an inspired gift to speak in front of hundreds, even thousands of diverse people, and to hold them spellbound with personal anecdotes and stories (like excellent teachers often do), and is especially skilled at sprinkling in delightful and humorous verbal zingers of love, wisdom, understanding, and caring.

» Though Janet's sister, Lynn, never spoke in front of such large groups as Janet was able to do, whenever she did have a small captive audience she, too, would often have them "rolling in the aisles" with laughter by merely mimicking her mother's cadence, rhythms, and feel for sarcastic zingers.
» I also want to thank Lynn, here, because it was when she and Janet were together sharing memories that Janet's story started to become so much more complete and compelling for me, and where I realized it simply must be told.
» It was also with Lynn, where we all realized more about how much my personal, highly-sensitive nature, to almost any level of zinger, coupled with my "Minnesota-nice" upbringings, clashed with their back history filled with cutting and sarcastic zingers. Another evidence of our uniqueness as an *"odd couple"*.

Additionally, I believe that my willingness to carefully listen to Janet, with unconditional love and faith in her stories and her perspectives, has been helpful and important for her. I am likewise very grateful to her, for her wisdom, understanding, love and support despite my many odd personal traits and struggles. We now share a common history of struggles in the face of an immense popular opposition, where everybody around us seemed ready and engaged in piling on, and we were usually left to find a way through it, alone. Until we found each other.

The struggles you will read about next were killing me. I mean every part of me, even the parts I didn't yet know about myself. But, because they helped me connect to Janet, it has made all of the difference. I could not have survived those coming struggles. I certainly could not have written this or any other book.

Now I am realizing more that they actually are the core of the book, and they are the foundation of how our *"odd couple"* relationship forms such a powerful and influential story. Separated, we were both vulnerable "mockingbirds". But, together we eventually started finding more effective ways to 'kill' the pushy Mocking - Birds; 'killing them with genuine patience and kindness'.

Like that of the remarkable man, Job, told about in the Book of Job, in the Bible's Old Testament. Kindness is free, but it often takes lots of time and patience before it starts to really take effect.

IRONIES WITHIN RELIGION: A SUPPOSED BALM FOR THE WEAK (OR THE WEAK MINDED?)

> ***Warning:*** *The next few subsections contain details about religions, churches, faith, worship, including some negative bigotry (religious zingers) and the unnecessary and sordid hurts and damage that those caused. These details come from our very personal viewpoints and perspectives. Me, having been caught alone much of this time, in the middle of 40 years of impossible struggles with these things (with almost nobody close to me, except Janet, even trying to listen or understand my perspective). Some of you probably already dislike organized religion in general, so in your case, I apologize and recommend that you skip the rest of this chapter entirely.*
>
> *Some of you might feel that my perspective is biased, and I suppose that is true, and that I need to admit that I have biases as everybody does. However, I promise you, with all of my heart, that my intention is* not *in any way meant to be negative towards anybody else's faith or unbelief or church, religion, or worship. I strongly believe that these things make up the most deeply held parts of ourselves, and should always be supported and encouraged, and never subjected to negative judgements or assumptions from outsiders. You may judge my outward behaviors (and to a certain extent, you should) but never try to judge another person's faith, or deep spiritual beliefs. In fact, this chapter illustrates many heartbreaking aspects of why this is so true.*

"OUT OF THE MOUTH OF INNOCENT BABES." (SEE PSALMS 8:2, MATTHEW 21:16, 11:25).

Janet had very early, even at five years old, found that religion provided a needed peace for her and Lynn throughout their tumultuous childhood stresses. Don and Vera had grown up during the Great Depression years when many rural farm families had to pitch in everything they could just to keep afloat, or even survive it. So, even though their families had traditions of faith and worship, church meetings and worship had been mostly put off during their childhood Great Depression years.

Nevertheless, they decided to join the Lutheran church near their neighborhood in Carmel, Indiana. Janet, in particular, was willing to faithfully beg for it, and always dressed herself and Lynn to get them to church (and Sunday school, or vacation Bible school), even when Mommy and Daddy weren't quite up to it, which was often. "Je-sus Christ, Janet, you and your sister can walk your own selves up to that goddamned church and back".

Janet and Lynn would often sing songs and liturgies from church when they were alone together. They even had a favorite game where they took turns being the donkey (named Joseph) and Doc (the dachshund) was "Baby Jesus", while the other got to play Mary and hold the baby Jesus all wrapped up in a swaddling blanket. Doc didn't like it nearly as much as they did, but he always played along anyway.

Janet's determination continued and her faith grew as the years passed. Particularly during confirmation prep classes, from grades seven through nine, she developed a strong knowledge and love for the Bible, and often felt a confirming witness of the Spirit inside herself that her efforts in that direction were very important and right.

This repeated spiritual witness is significant, because Janet was learning more about God, and how to receive divine peace and comfort. It was almost always tied to study in the Bible, or worship, or other actions directly related to such.

Early in her marriage, Janet knew that she would need to find a church, but she was very unsure whether John would approve or participate. John's family were Methodists and his parents and older siblings sometimes attended, so she often gently invited him, "Let's try attending a church this Sunday." He kept strictly refusing, but she still thought that she would join a nice Methodist (or Lutheran) group anyway, and hoped that he would participate eventually, once they had children enrolled in such activities.

Then, something totally unexpected occurred that was to uniquely and profoundly affect and change Janet's life and her story, literally forever...

AN IRRATIONAL BUT POPULAR OPPOSITION.

Two young missionaries from the Church of Jesus Christ of Latter-day Saints knocked on their apartment door in a northern suburb of Pittsburgh, PA one afternoon while John was away at work. The message that they told was very unique, and Janet thought the two nineteen year old boys from Utah were incredibly polite, respectful, and innocent about it. And, since she was a newly graduated and certified high school English teacher, she had a lot of current experience with high school students only a year or so younger (about sixteen to eighteen years old), especially given the many modern cultural changes affecting young people in the mid-1970s.

Janet was a smoker back then, and she often drank mixed alcoholic cocktails or beer with John and friends. She still planned to join the Methodists or Lutherans, but she was intrigued by these Mormon boys and their remarkably unique message, so she decided to listen and discuss with them a little more. They always kept their visits and discussions brief, between thirty minutes and an hour. Early on, they tried hard to catch times when John would be there. John, however, rigidly rejected any and all friendships from them, or chances to listen to their messages.

Janet decided she really needed to at least try to find out exactly where these Mormons were so wrong. After all, they clearly must be completely wrong given how intensely unpopular and hated they seemed to be. So, she dug hard into every claim for or against them (especially every Biblical issue), and she tested the two young men as hard as she could with questions and observations. Besides the pamphlets and info those boys gave her, she was quickly given stacks of anti-Mormon literature by her parents, all linked to prevalent anti-cult ministries.

If she was impressed and surprised that she just could not find anything seriously or inexplicably wrong with them in any area (other than the incredible amounts of innocence and worldly naivety) she eventually became much more surprised at how negatively people around her reacted to her personal investigations, and how long and aggressively they kept up the wide-variety of negative pressures on her to stop investigating. She was also very surprised at understanding the Bible (especially the Old Testament - on prophecies and the future of Israel; including all twelve tribes, not just the Jews -- the lone tribe of Judah) in very important and comprehensively agreeable ways she never had even noticed or knew existed before these intense investigations, because Janet had always tried hard to fully know and fully understand the Bible.

Additionally, Janet repeatedly found those negative scoffers connected to her amazingly ignorant of even the most basic issues involved in her sincere investigations, or even within their own mocking and negative accusations (always tracing to the same tired-issues or details raised by the same anti-cult ministries). Because they so uncharacteristically "excluded" Mormons and seemingly so many others from their unnecessarily harsh, narrow, and 'exclusive' interpretation of Christian salvation.

Note: This is Janet's personal story. I am intentionally not chronicling all of the details of these disputes or differences, or trying to convince you which side is more correct, for you.

Please decide for yourself about the content-details of this opposition. I will merely note how pushy and narrow its interpretation of Christian-salvation was repeatedly directed towards us, mostly against us. But why us? (innocent investigators) And, why over such a long time?

*We have never disputed that the LDS are somewhat different from all other Christian groups. However, our forty five years of intense investigations kept consistently confirming to us that every slight difference (or issue) cited, in fact, makes them **more** Biblical, thus **more** Christian; and much more open, respectful and inclusive towards others' faith and beliefs, no matter what they might be.*

Surprisingly, during our entire investigations, not one of the differences or issues raised seemed to make them less Biblical, from our intensely studied perspectives and observations. Ironically, such differences were even prophesied to occur. (For example, the continuing Protestant Reformations have identified and adjusted for some of these very same issues, and the more recent Great Awakening revivals have identified and adjusted for others.)

Do these slight-differences mean that all other Christian groups are completely wrong or completely non-Christian, from our perspective? Of course not. At least no more than the slight differences between each of the other Christian groups makes them more or less non-Christian, or wrong than any other.

The difference that agreed most powerfully with Biblical history and writings is that within both the Old Testament and the New Testament writings, whenever serious apostate differences did arise amongst God's chosen covenant people, they were never fully resolved by popular councils or universities; they were always identified and adjusted for by "authentic and authoritatively called" prophets or lead apostles (often associated with "miraculous-visits" from Jehovah or His Angelic messengers). And, the existing apostate religious and political leaders always resented, rejected, and eventually killed these authentic and authoritatively called prophets or apostles, which also was prophesied to occur in the last-days.

Invariably, those harsh rejections and persecutions would ironically help strengthen a few of these Biblical people to become more devoutly honest and true to the previously-diluted essence and core of their faith and covenants in God. Thus, God was slowly and intentionally using those oppositions and persecutions for His important purposes during Biblical-times, as He also does today.

Teaching the controversy: I think it is helpful and important to note here, in my humble opinion; DON'T TRY TO TEACH ANY CONTROVERSIAL DIFFERENCES TO CLOSE FRIENDS OR LOVED ONES. **Not by yourself, anyway.** Use the full-time missionaries for that part of any teaching. In fact, you should probably not even be present when those most unique and controversial differences and messages are taught, because they are so controversial, people need to be completely free to question them, and decide for themselves, completely unencumbered by any feelings of obligation or respect, as per those shared by close family or friendships. In fact, that is exactly why I am not detailing any of those most controversial messages and aspects in this book. -- It complicates and muddles-up the other goals and objectives I have for writing these stories and this book.

COMPANIONS ON THE LORD'S ERRAND.

As time passed, many different sets of young missionaries (some boy sets, but mostly girls) visited and taught Janet, often bringing another member along as well. Besides intensely testing their teachings, Janet tested each missionary. Even though she found them eminently similar to her highschool students and normal in all other ways, she *always* noticed a strangely authentic spiritual "presence or gift" about them, which always added an extraordinary and impressive maturity and effectiveness to their actions and teachings (clearly above what a normal youth of their age and education could perform). Yet more than this, she could also always sense or "feel" this subtle peaceful presence about them.

Janet pondered and prayed about it extensively. She finally discerned that it had to be an unusual and special companionship of the Holy Ghost. Her ponderings confirmed to her in multiple ways that these extraordinary and impressive aspects of these young missionaries were simply unexplainable in any other way. Her carefully and deeply tested sample size, back then, was easily ten to twenty; now it's several hundred.

Janet was always more than a bit disappointed when the missionaries had to leave. As I mentioned, they always kept their visits short. But, somehow that made Janet study and pray that much harder. And, as she looks back at those times of diligent Biblical study and prayers, she remembers multiple times when she experienced intense spiritual confirmations. Per many private discussions between us, Janet's spiritual confirmations (personal religious experiences) back then seem to compare fairly closely to those that I had during my early investigations, by myself.

> *Where sometimes my whole body, soul, and especially my mind seemed to tingle and sometimes even shiver with lasting and unforgettable joy, and with more subtle but profound kinds of – deep "burning" confirmations and possibilities for lasting, and maybe even endless different manifestations of peace and blissful happiness from God, like I had never before even dreamed were possible.*
>
> *To this day, so many years later, I will never forget those feelings. And, I continue to periodically find re-confirmations of that subtle but deep "burning" that was ignited deep within my very-bones so many years ago, as I study, fast, and pray upon those similar questions and answers I was seeking so diligently way back then.*

However, the reality of the punishing and isolating disapproval and negativity from John, family, and friends would always quickly come back, leaving Janet feeling intense frustration, sorrow, and loneliness, because none of them would or could seem to listen or give her any chance to explain. Janet remembers many times being encompassed by hopeless doubts. Even after first considering that these unique teachings must be true, she could not escape the overwhelming reality that it could never really happen for her. The enormously heavy hand of suppression and disapproval by her parents, then John, and now everyone else around her seemed to be committed to crushing her newfound faith and hopes. They would just never relent.

They seemed to be genuinely afraid for her and hurt or embarrassed that she would get involved in such a hated and unpopular group, and so excluded from their accepted and popular societies. They seemed especially afraid and embarrassed of what it might eventually lead to. They were often angry and quick to blame her for such foolishness, yet they would never, ever listen or consider her side of such things. She simply was never going to be able to do this, or even freely consider this.

Nevertheless, Janet as a vulnerable young child had already developed and proven incredible patience and faith that truth and love somehow miraculously prevails in the end. So, instead of arguing with any of them, or giving up, she quietly and humbly went forward with her responsibilities, somehow confident that things would work out someday.

Over the next seventeen years, the negative reactions from others persisted and even escalated until Janet's marriage had no normal or fair chance whatsoever of surviving. But ironically, during that entire time, the main reasoning and rationale for their negative reactions never even existed yet...

Janet was never an officially recorded LDS church member, during any of these years. She was always merely a curious - but "non-member" investigator, never baptized, never fully active or fully "tithed", never attended any temples, never did any full time mission work. Although she taught and prayed with her girls from the Bible, she never taught them any LDS-specific information.

In fact, she didn't attend any LDS worship until years after that first missionary visit at their apartment, and would often break off any activities and investigations to see if that might soften John's or other people's negative reactions. But invariably, even such break offs and inactivity never seemed to fully ease those negative reactions. The pushy people most focused on these particular negatives just could not let go of it for some unexplained reasons. The rest, who were maybe less sure of the "evil cult" claims, seemed comfortably resigned to just "look the other way" and pretend that maybe one or more of the pushy people genuinely knew and wanted the best for Janet.

But some of these "pushy people" were far too overly self-assured, unfair, selfish, and sometimes even ignorant jerks about it. Of course none of them knew much about Janet's harsh-abusive childhood. If they had, they might have been more careful, tolerant, and maybe even sympathetic to her search for genuine truth and love (especially within families and marriage). And, especially since the childhood damage to her psyche had so unsuspectedly contributed to so many of her current woes, per her poor choice of John as her current spouse.

You see, LDS missionaries and leaders had strict policies against baptizing any married woman if any opposition existed in her husband, or in other words, without his full and clear consent. And, in Janet's case, that would never happen (see the short-story about that in The Epilogue at the very end of this book). But so many LDS people kept presuming that her "non-member" status was her own choice, or her own fault. Eventually, Janet simply gave up trying to explain it to most of them.

There is a pathetically funny scene in the movie-comedy, "Airplane", where a woman is so fearfully 'panicked' that the stewardess tries to roughly shake her out of her hysteria. Then a large businessman behind the stewardice taps her shoulder and calmly says, "Here, let me handle this," as he proceeds to more violently shake and slap the woman. Then the pilot stops him and proceeds to shake the woman and repeatedly slap her even harder and more, followed by a hard-slapping Nun, and others with boxing-gloves, bats, and wrenches, all waiting their turn in line to take a crack at this poor innocent woman, because if the stewardess can't shake the "hysteria" out of her - by God they're somehow more than willing to take a good hard shot at it, for everyone's sake.

Well anyway, that's how it felt sometimes to Janet, when so many pushy people seemed to be lining up to do her the favor of stopping her from considering or investigating baptism with the missionaries over such a long time. Which investigation and baptism, they were all somehow so extremely-sure needed to be stopped for everyone's best interests.

Nobody (except Lynn) knew Janet's childhood abuse history, even John. The few times she ever tried to mention her childhood abuse, others just didn't seem to get it, especially John. Lynn always lived far away, and during their few times together, John had absolutely no interest in knowing or understanding such a financially-failed "throw away" portion of Janet's family (US military were notoriously underpaid during this post-Vietnam era). Eventually, Janet simply gave up trying to explain it to anyone, even LDS people.

And somehow, various pushy-jerks would repeatedly arise and pick-up on her vulnerability to abuse and mistreatment. Because if her own husband and parents didn't care about her or defend her, maybe they might be able to take some kind of predatory advantage there too.

These pushy, judgemental people were always vastly underestimating Janet's overall life-strength and resolve. And, their irrational bigotry can best be compared to the totally irrational anti-Semitism which somehow keeps raising its ugly hate-driven head, for reasons nobody can ever fully explain, even despite vigilant and worldwide watches ever since the horrible Nazi "Holocaust".

DEEPER OBSERVATIONS AND TESTIMONY

By odd coincidence, both of Janet's first trial visits to LDS Sunday worship (though several long months apart) happened to be "fast and testimony meetings" which are held one Sunday each month. Janet was unusually touched and impressed by the humble overall-Spirit of these meetings. Was everyone in the entire congregation really and honestly genuinely-fasting together, even the children? And were they all really and honestly giving a generous fast-offering to assist the poor and the needy (based on actual savings from the skipped meals)?

Janet had read scriptures about the power of universal fasting in the Old Testament, and she had once been similarly impressed by the Ramadan fasting and prayers of an admired Muslim friend. But she had never actually experienced anything like this. Not amongst Christians. There was something refreshingly powerful, and genuinely spiritual about both those meetings, and those innocent and sincere testimonies.

To this day, some 40 years later, Janet and I have continued to find each of these unique fast and testimony meetings wonderfully and meekly genuine, and we have yet to find anything remotely like it, amongst any other group or people. And surprisingly, most of the prominent sermons, talks, and classroom lessons on the remaining Sundays are given representatively by ordinary members of the congregation, especially the women and children.

Per our early observations, most of the leading men seemed focused on clerical and administrative matters, so their wives, children, and others could maximize their opportunities to actually serve the people in the congregation as the up-front teachers, speakers, and leaders. These aspects have never ceased to amaze us even now because they always create a miraculous kind of unity and efficiency not found anywhere else. And absolutely nobody gets paid for any of these incredible services or talents, which again is forever amazing and super-efficient.

Another amazing aspect of this unique organizational design is how it somehow contributes to miraculous uniformity and unity throughout the entire church worldwide. We have now observed and participated in worship and activities from the smallest branches in remote northern Minnesota or Mexico, to huge big-city congregations out east or in Utah.

In each of these diverse locations and settings we were repeatedly amazed at how similar the actual content and teachings happened to be. No other church or group comes close to the overall uniformity and unity found throughout the mainline Church of Jesus Christ of Latter-day Saints (although many such groups/ or churches are very good, they ALWAYS take on uniquely different flavors from their local-leader(s) thus quickly losing overall uniformity, and that rare-precious unity). That's a fact based upon our two long and diverse lifetimes of experiences in these things, gained across many diverse churches and cultures.

OF STABLE LOVING FAMILIES.

Considering Janet's childhood, it is not surprising that she was attracted to the genuine unity and closeness found within many Mormon families. Mormon families are generally considered to be of high character and excellent at child-rearing, even by the most skeptical of outsiders.

Some of the best families that she encountered traced to the early Mormon-Pioneers and many of their family-lines came directly from people practicing plural marriage until 130-years ago when polygamy was strictly abolished and forbidden by the church. Janet having had no previous experience with LDS, was especially interested in observing these descendants of polygamy since it was the basis for so much of the modern mocking, false presumptions, and criticisms she had heard.

All of these people (descendants of polygamy) seemed especially grateful for the great sacrifices of their Pioneer-ancestors, including the huge sacrifice of submission to their religious calling in such marriage. None of them want to go back to such days. In fact, none of their ancestors wanted it back then. It was always a huge sacrifice, and a hardship that nobody had ever asked for.

Apparently, it was never as people seem so quick to assume. Only a very small portion of families practiced it (less than 2%), even back then. Those rare families were never forced, but they were always specially "chosen" and called to such marriages. They didn't get to choose it for themselves, in fact, many of the wives "chosen" for each family were older single women who had no other chance for needed shelter within the harsh frontier environment and economy. They would otherwise have been destitute on the harsh frontier landscape with little or no real support around them.

I won't try to describe exactly how they practiced or managed all of the intricacies of such marriage way back then. But, let's quickly look at the resulting quality of families and individuals who have come from those Pioneer families, in comparison to other families, or to other groups practicing polygamy in their own different ways.

For instance, several diverse groups have since broken off from the mainline LDS because they wanted to keep practicing polygamy. Have any of those groups or families found success or prosperity, by any measure? No, in fact, we repeatedly find terrible tragedy and unhappiness growing and progressing amongst them. Likewise amongst many other polygamist groups around the world today, and throughout history.

Conversely, the few mainline LDS families who practiced plural marriage between 1840s-1890 seem to have somehow produced a "dream team" of some of the finest, most loving, serving, and refined families and individuals to be found anywhere today, or anytime in modern history. Among these high achieving families and individuals are many famous and successful billionaires, businessmen, Governors, Senators, church leaders, highly educated university leaders, and great writers, speakers, artists, and musicians. In fact, by odd coincidence, Janet became well acquainted with several incredible individuals amongst them very early on in her investigations (see The Epilogue, at the very end of this book).

Janet and I both feel strongly that these people and families coming from these early Pioneer-polygamist families are further evidence and proof that God uses extreme hardships and persecutions of unpopular cursings to test and refine his people. In fact, we feel a particularly strong kinship with these people because besides being befriended by them, our cursings and persecutions seem somewhat similar from our personal stories and perspectives.

THE POPULAR (ANTI) OPPOSITION: SO UBIQUITOUS AND NEVER ENDING, IT'S NOW CLEARLY INDISPUTABLE AND UNDENIABLE.

This never-ending popular anti/ opposition did not make rational sense to Janet, then or now. And, because she very intensely and responsibly studied all of it and found it filled with serious holes and half truths, it was effectively helping to convince and confirm to her more fully that the remarkable unique message those first boys told simply must be true. Besides, whether the opposition was even partially right or wrong, didn't really matter. Janet got repeated and undeniable spiritually sure-witnesses within herself, which has ever since then - turned out to be most important for her personal faith decisions and directions.

Surely millions of other LDS-investigators (now converts) have experienced almost the exact same kind of pushy oppositions that Janet did here, and surely these oppositions made many of them stronger and more determined, also. The big difference is Janet's humble patience and perseverance over such an incredibly long period of decades (which has proven to crush most), and also for so long before her own baptism and membership were even allowed. Then she marries me, who had experienced eighteen years of similar oppositions from my family, wife, and friends. Now it's been an additional 27 years of us together, with people (especially close family) still vastly underestimating our combined patience, faith, and perseverance in this (as an unusually chosen and special "odd couple").

By the way, TENS of millions of non-converted former LDS-investigators (or at least curious-listeners, not strong enough to persevere it) also still exist -- who chose not to join because they were also wounded or harmed by such similar "pushy and un-ending flack" about it. Thus they ALSO now stand as supplemental witnesses of this popular opposition. So, please don't anybody try to deny or argue that this pushy and irrational popular opposition (especially focused on us most vulnerable investigators) does not exist, or that it does not harm innocent vulnerable people. Actually, hundreds of millions (maybe billions) worldwide now have either experienced it themselves, or observed this popular opposition happening to others to some degree or another. Given the strong sense of "fairness" shared by all humans, especially innocent children, such popular persecutions may be about to someday massively "backfire" on those pushy persecutors, and counter-cult ministries.

The biggest anomaly with Janet and I together is, we now have this uniquely difficult and long 45-year story together and a book published about it (as a particularly patient and longsuffering*"odd couple"*), which gives us a unique forum to communicate about it like very few others ever in these modern times, especially given the added links to the horrible hypocrisies of Janet's incredibly harsh and abusive parents and childhood. We want to in turn help others get their stories told, or finally fulfilled in some way, whether big or small.

THE BIBLE BELT.

During her long-hard investigations, Janet found college level extension classes in Biblical-seminary (both Old and New Testaments). She became so interested and inspired by these new insights, that she completed all four classes, and then audited and completed each class a second time for a total of eight college level scripture classes. Comparing these studies with the literature from the anti-cult ministries and from the LDS missionaries helped Janet to uniquely understand and zero in on much more of a fullness of truths and wisdom available in the Bible than any of her previous studies in confirmation classes had provided, or from the extremely negative bias (and shallow, exaggerated half-truths) from the anti cult ministries.

These Bible studies also awakened in her incredible levels of hope and faith that many more hidden levels of answers and solutions exist here in these Biblical scriptures. And given the hypocrisy, abuse, and times of her youth, Janet was extremely and highly motivated to sincerely and faithfully search and find any such genuine and authentic answers.

In fact, she now has a half dozen Bibles with markings on almost every page and chapter as evidence of her diligence in the scriptures throughout her life. She has many favorite verses and chapters, where the Spirit has "witnessed" to her heart and mind (many times, in many different ways) that these things are true and important for her. Even today, Janet and I are always searching the Bible for more answers, reading and re-reading, and amazingly she continues to find new answers hidden within the embedded patterns, symbols, and mysteries of the parables, stories, and prophecies of the Bible.

When a friend invited Janet to attend worship at her fast-growing Bible Church, Janet respectfully went and joyfully worshiped and prayed with her. And, when she brought her popular Bible Church minister to Janet to warn her about Mormons, Janet politely agreed to listen. But after hearing the same tired-issues repeated (tracing back to those same counter-cult ministries), Janet asked, "Can you tell me, when was your Bible Church started?"

"Two years ago."

"And, how many Mormons have you known?"

"Oh, I've never actually met any Mormons."

"So, you're the head of this fairly new Bible Church, and have never even met an actual member of The Church of Jesus Christ located right here within your neighborhood. Now, if I want to see and know more about your new Bible Church I believe I should of course come here and ask you. But, who do you think I should ask, if I want to *really* know the full-details about the actual authoritative Church of Jesus Christ of Latter-day Saints?"

Suddenly, they had nothing much more to say, or to respond to that simple but pertinent question.

I do not want to judge any particular church or the people in it. Janet and I still know and respect many others who attend churches similar to that one, especially the importance, time, and leadership they place on Formal Bible study-groups and classes. We have participated in many such Bible study-groups and have always enjoyed and admired that aspect. We have always believed in a strong "literal" and "fundamentalist" view of the importance of the Bible and its core teachings and prophecies.

However, we will never see pushy politics or political contentions over controversial moral-issues as the main role the church and its influence and leadership of members should focus on. Rather, each member should be encouraged to choose and make their own independent decisions, votes, or other actions on such politically hot-button moral-issues and disputes.

Unfortunately, we kept finding pushy and outspoken leaders within such Bible study groups and churches heavily influenced, or significantly linked to side associations with specific Christian fundamentalist schools, colleges, seminaries, publishers, and "parachurch" ministries broadcast on radio or telecast, which have been chasing after popular and sensational political advantages and promotions by getting increasingly controversial and divisive. Many of these most prominent evangelical "parachurch" and radio ministries or programs have been politically focusing on the popular exaggerated extremes within controversies between the recent politics of extreme Christian fundamentalism vs. more moderate and established mainline Christianity or politics.

DEVALUING MODERATE-INCLUSIVE CHRISTIANITY.

Many moderate Christian leaders have warned that such pushy extremes and controversies tend to unwisely create more division, and less unity and collaboration within the overall Christian movement. They warn that such focus is proven to subtly devalue and delegitimize the faith, salvation, or even the patriotism of other Christians, merely because of minor differences and unsubstantiated opinions (Yes, that's clearly un-Christlike).

These moderate-leaders point to many ruthless and pushy purges that have occurred, usually against more moderate and progressive Christian leaders and groups. They point out that the political focus of such controversies reveal that the motivation is not actually on gospel, Bible, or religion, but much more on the ambitious quest to obtain or maintain greater conservative political power and influence, and that they are willing to allow or use exaggerated misinformation, even pushy threats, and fear, whether real or just condoned. They point to the many radio and telecast ministries and personalities that have risen to great heights of prominence and power, and somehow remained there despite repeated episodes of serious controversies and even criminal scandals. See the history of many popular televangelists and ministries that have self-sabotaged and self-destructed due to their own selfish hypocrisy. Yet somehow they keep on rolling.*

**Note: Who are the "They"? Who are these unnamed "moderate Christian leaders" who I seem to be quoting? Do you want a list of referenced quotes from just the last year (2021)? Or maybe you would prefer a list over the last 10, or maybe the last 50 years? I assure you, the referenced quotes citing concerns about the issues listed above would be substantial. Or, maybe you would like to see a much larger and comprehensive list of Christians, or even just recognized Christian leaders who have not yet been quoted (at least not in referenced publication), but would be willing to sign a universal petition of concern about the issues listed above.*

But why has nobody effectively promoted or acted on such a list or petition? Maybe they are all more than just a little bit leery of those exaggerated misinformation tactics, even threats, and fear, whether real or just condoned, especially on social media tweets, postings and commentaries, that they have seen repeatedly used against those who dared to question these issues.

I mention these concerns, because they are so close to what Janet and I have quietly suffered and observed for so long about the pushy anti-cult, or counter cult ministries. Using narrowly exaggerated stereotypes, labels, and slur-terms (like non-Christian "cults"), they subtly tend to demonize and dehumanize innocent and vulnerable people, thus hurting them and their children as our examples clearly prove.

And like so many other pushy populist leaders and groups who have gained status and power by tapping into existing stereotypes and even hatred against vulnerable scapegoats, their popular "hay day" always eventually unravels and comes to an embarrassing and premature end. Especially if their vulnerable scapegoats have enough rare patience and "spunky" courage to prove them wrong through their long-suffering examples (see Janet and me, as "*odd couple*").

WHAT WOULD JESUS DO?

Let's remember. Jesus always found ways to recognize and include the worth of everyone; especially the scapegoats and underdogs, the poor and sick, even the sinners, tax-collectors, publicans, and Samaritans.

He attracted huge crowds, and included everyone in his teachings and blessings.

But Jesus wisely avoided the over-zealous and pushy political disputes and opinions of His day, from the wicked and worldwide Roman and Greek Empires, to local King Herod issues, to the religious disputes between the Scribes, Chief-Priests, Pharisees, Sadducees, Essenes, or the violent local Jewish-zealots and revolts. Whenever intentionally confronted about such issues, He ingeniously avoided them once saying, "Render therefore unto Caesar the things which are Caesar's, and to God the things that are God's." -- Matt 22:22, Mark 12:17, Luke 20:25.

After Jesus's healings and miraculously feeding the multitudes, many Jewish followers tried to forcefully make Him their earthly King. But their supposedly grand ideas for Him were selfishly flawed so He escaped their pushy counterfeit ideas and King-worship to work out His own more meaningful, gentle, and lasting pathway.

Although "His Way" of ministering and deeply converting each person separately, one-by-one, line-by-line, and precept-upon-precept is much slower, gentler, and much less dramatic or showy than the mega-crusade-events or the pushy popular political rallies or revival-events. But, the effects of those popular but very-fickle mega-events and rallies are so shallow and short-lived. They don't last. It's repeatedly been proven now, they just don't last or stay very long.

CHRONIC PROBLEMS IN CONTEMPORARY CHRISTIAN WORSHIP MUSIC.

I am no expert on the loud new contemporary worship music, but at least some of it seems inappropriately irreverent and problematic to me. *"The Lord is in His holy temple: let all the earth keep silence (and reverence) before Him"* (Habakuk 2:20).

The Bible has dozens of other similar verses clearly calling for deep reverence and quiet respect in the Lord's house, and while worshiping in His Holy presence. Yes, we sing sacred praises to Him (sacred hymns), but for the last several hundreds of years the sacred hymns and the music-instrumentals used to accompany them have always been designed to evoke quiet-sacred and reverent feelings of holiness and solemnity. Only in these last fifty years or so (especially recently), has Christian worship started deviating from that. Again, I am certainly no expert, but those who have studied to become the most-informed experts on these trends are finding serious problems. More information and links about this can be found in chapter 12 of this book.

Again, I mention these problems and concerns, because the unwise and unfair judgments, bigotry, and hypocrisy they illustrate are so close to what Janet and I have quietly suffered and observed for so long about the pushy anti-cult, or counter-cult ministries which kept coming against us and our children personally in one pushy way or another. Always using quick, easy, but very shallow and diluted-down rationale and tactics to discount and negate any of our personal feelings or perspectives.

WHAT'S THE MATTER? CAN'T TAKE A JOKE?

Recently the slogan "Let's Go Brandon" has become a popular and humorous meme for many pushy political-conservatives. It originated at a recent NASCAR race in Alabama. While the winner (named Brandon) was being interviewed, the telecast reporter stated, "You can hear the chants from the crowd, 'Let's go, Brandon!'" However, the crowd was actually taunting current US President, Joe Biden, with chants using an extremely vulgar slur term. It's unclear how the reporter actually misheard the chant, but footage of the interview was placed on social media and rapidly went viral.

Apparently this slogan has now been cropping up everywhere even at many church and worship events. Which illustrates how such vulgar and pushy slurs and stereotypes can become so quickly and powerfully perpetuated within our popular and fickle culture today.

Maybe it's time to finally drive a "wooden stake" through the heart of this horrific kind of mean-spirited public mocking and bullying. Maybe we can finally take a look at ourselves, and once and for all stop these pushy slurs and stereotypes, which make us all look like ignorant bigots to the rest of the world and even to our own children and grandchildren.

I doubt that most of us yet have the courage to change this, but maybe this book can help just a little bit. Kindness is free, so let's some of us go out there and kill'em with kindness.

CHAPTER 7

STRUGGLING TOGETHER

MORE ON MY PERSONAL INVESTIGATIONS AND STRUGGLES.

HALF-BREED REFUGEES?

I apologize for this headline and using such a derogatory racially charged slur term as "half-breed". I could not find any other term that fits our stories as well as this term. I will explain more about this as these stories fill in.

Side Note: The following stories will probably sound exaggerated to some. Please understand that I am merely trying to capture and tell the much misunderstood minority perspectives of those caught beneath the pushy viewpoints of those siding and piling on with the popular opposition. I have never intended to vengefully blame anybody in particular about this. I merely want to tell these stories to help us all understand and respect each other better. Kindness is free, so let's kill'em with kindness. As Janet's current husband, and main chronicler of her important stories, I feel a special duty to cover and explain these damages to her and others like her and me, and the many children affected also.

I bumped into Janet in the church hallway one very cold winter Minnesota evening for me. It was just a few weeks after my wife had unexpectedly insisted on a break from our almost seventeen-year marriage, along with rigid insistence that I had to move out, even though I clearly had no other social life to turn to at that time. All of my family and friends had by then in some way joined and effectively piled on together with the popular opposition against me, despite my sacrifices and pleadings for understanding. For many years previous, I had dared not even mention any of my investigations or faith findings or feelings without my wife implicitly gathering another supposed-expert individual or committee unfairly accusing and confirming me as a mentally weak and defective evil cultist; or even a supposed fanatical lunatic.

I was devastated. I felt deeply shocked and betrayed, even by God, *especially* by God. Why was I being unjustly punished again, for my quiet-patience and innocent faith in God, when others were being religiously rewarded for their pushy opposition, and far less sincere faith and sacrifice? I didn't know what to do. I had invested absolutely everything I could into my marriage, and my fragile little family, including my two young boys and one little daughter.

I couldn't think straight. My mind kept going around in circles. Several times I would be driving somewhere, and before long, I realized I was ten or twenty miles past my intended destination, and somehow couldn't remember anything in between. I eventually got a prescription for anti-depression pills, because I just couldn't stop my mind from this "uncontrollable racing" during that tragic time period.

I didn't know Janet then, but she knew a little about me through others at church. And, she understood a lot more about what I had been going through for the past 17 years of a marriage stressed by over-reactions to my innocent investigations of the Church of Jesus Christ of Latter-day Saints, having just endured so much of that herself.

Only about nine months earlier, I had taken a desperate and unusual opportunity to unexpectedly travel by myself, over 350 miles round trip, on short notice to plead with a gathering of my family that some hidden ominous betrayals seemed to be happening with my wife behind my back, which might seriously and tragically damage me, my marriage, and my little children.

I was hoping they would be concerned enough for me, my marriage, and my vulnerable little children; that they might take a different perspective, and really listen to me for a change. And, since some of them regularly seemed to speak to my wife behind my back about me, I was hoping to find a way to turn that around and maybe find a way to fix the damages caused by such betrayals.

Instead of carefully listening to me, and letting the family carefully listen and respond to me at this desperately critical time, one dominant person had to scold me again about how foolish and wrong I was, subtly implying how they all knew so much more than I did about what was really happening with me, my wife, and the evil cult. The other family there should have stopped it, or defended me from this popular (but cruel and untrue) opposition, as they should have done with dozens of other times and peoples. But, they just didn't seem to be able to stand up against the popular opposition or maybe to understand or care enough to really listen to me. So, they let it happen again and group-insisted that it must be my fault, again.

My family, including my wife, were always communicating behind my back, and were so absolutely sure of themselves and their agreed-upon conclusions that they all needed to be united in not listening or cooperating with me. They would subtly taunt me about the total family consensus they had achieved (including my parents, four sisters, their husbands, and numerous uncles, aunts, cousins, and many close family friends).

Supposedly, because I was so foolishly indoctrinated into the "cult", and that the cult's only intention (and mine) was to trick others into the cult (totally wrong and unfair, even now after 40 years, as I will never be as fully culturalized as they were accusing me of). And, as much as I tried -- now over forty years -- to gently and respectfully explain and demonstrate otherwise, they would just never, ever listen or consider anything else. They evidently will never understand or acknowledge how much pain, suffering, sacrifice, and damage to marriages, families, and children such narrow-minded bigotry has caused innocent investigators like Janet and me.

From my perspective, my daughter Anna is the only person from my own family to ever listen to me about this, or even consider that the popular opposition might be even a little bit biased and wrong about my personal beliefs and convictions. But, even that was only after Anna became twenty three years old, and despite the obvious great risk and crushing stresses, initiated and worked out her own sincere and personal investigation without me even knowing about it. She wisely waited patiently until she had moved out of her mom's house, and surprised everyone, especially me and Janet, then living and working far away in New York.

WHY WOULD THEY REJECT, AND NOT EVEN LISTEN TO SUCH A GENTLE AND LOVING INVITE?

As for the other matter, if my intention was ever to subtly trick others into the cult, why then did we not ever teach or even allow our own children to be taught in childhood, when most people would *scream, kick, or kill* before even considering giving up that privilege? Why did we sacrifice our own worship, activities, and culturalization for so many years and even somewhat so now? Again, a privilege many people throughout history have justified massive wars and killing for.

Why are most of our own children, grandchildren, family and former close friends not in any way involved, or even remotely knowledgeable about such religion? If you asked them questions about LDS-religion, I mean dozens of the simplest most basic questions that even the newest investigators would know, or that 1st or 2nd grade LDS children know, or that 3rd graders have read themselves and could easily show you exactly where to find them about Jesus' witness within the Book of Mormon; they wouldn't have the faintest clue or even any regret or embarrassment about such ignorance. I know because although some of them brag and pretend to confidently know everything about the mainline Church of Jesus Christ of Latter-day Saints, I've had to just patiently bear their hurtful inaccuracies and hypocrisies for over 40 years.

And, why did Anna, after investigating and joining completely on her own accord, decide that she needed to totally refrain from ever even mentioning it within most family and friends? Perhaps she too felt heavily threatened, intimidated, and stressed until it seriously broke her.

And, why am I now writing an extensive book about these things, but likewise refraining from detailing any of those unique and specific content messages and teachings which most powerfully convinced Janet, Anna, and me to humbly start and continue investigating this very unique but unpopular church, along with so many other vulnerable scapegoats and underdogs?

And, why am I gently challenging and encouraging readers to find and tell their own independent stories, no matter what their faith or their politics; And only then inviting them to consider our stories of patience and courage as an example to help each of them, independently?

You see, for over forty years, whenever I would even mention or gently invite somebody to understand even a tiny-bit of my perspective on anything, I have been repeatedly gang-ridiculed and rudely accused of pushing my cult "insanity" on others. Usually, these strongest objections didn't even come from the person I gently spoke to. Usually, it was by one of the pushy-people mentioned earlier, who probably wasn't even there when I dared mention anything. I, personally, am glad for every one of those gentle invites or "mentionings" that I ever had the courage to gently offer. What kind of man would I be, or would I have been back then, if I had never even risked mentioning my most cherished and important thoughts and feelings.

Please don't shoot me again about my gentle attempts to explain or answer this pushy opposition. I know many hate how the mainline Church of Jesus Christ of Latter-day Saints continues to find listeners to its young 18-year old missionaries. But, that's not my fault.

My family and friends should not have continued to let so much pushy fear, ignorance, and embarrassments exist amongst themselves, and especially against me. We were NOT ever "tricked" into that "ingenious cult". Nobody is, and nobody ever has been "so-called tricked". From its very beginnings it's always been a very unpopular, serious, and often 'dangerous' commitment for anybody to make. Janet and I are just two simple ordinary examples of how hard and long it eventually might become for some who choose this pathway, especially in the heartland of America's proud Bible-belt.

Especially, for the most vulnerable of investigators, like we were, or we eventually became. Especially, for those whose own spouses and families opposed it as much as ours did over such a long-hard period of time.

Of course I don't expect or even want anybody to quickly or lightly join my opinions, church, or religion based upon a mere mention or simple "invite" from me. Nor do I expect or even want that from publishing or promoting this book. That is clearly not the subject or the purpose of this book, so shame on anyone saying that about me now, or back over those long forty years of unnecessary isolation and bigotry.

Let this entire book along with that long established forty-year record prove me innocent of those unfair accusations, now and forever. But, if you or anybody wants to push that old disproven argument, go ahead, knock yourself out. It will be nothing new to me and I promise you, it will probably help me promote and sell this book, especially within your own family and neighborhood. Kindness and patience is free, I will continue to kill'em with kindness.

We patiently waited over 45-years to finally tell this entire story in a comprehensive and indisputable way, because we both expected some will make those claims again. This book proves that these stories will now finally be heard, especially since thousands of past LDS-investigators and the missionaries who taught them are agreeing that they also saw such similar tactics from their experiences.

Side note: Please understand that I know that nobody is perfect or blameless in any of this. Blaming and shaming always has two sides and it is never right to not consider both sides of such issues.

The long history of religious proselytization has so often involved pushy coercion, bribery, or trickery; So I can understand how many people assume that ambitious LDS missionary outreach and efforts might or must involve at least some of the same.

Much of Latin-America was forced Catholic by pushy conquistadors and their missionary-priests. And, millions of Africans and Islanders were heavily coerced through bribery into baptism by various Protestant missionary groups.

Janet and I both testify that all of the outside pressures involved in our investigations were to stop us, rather than the missionaries quickly baptizing us just to increase their numbers. In fact, they wouldn't let Janet be baptized for 17-years, and they wouldn't let me and most others be baptized until strict objectives and spiritual qualifiers were met. God's true plan always prioritizes deep genuine faith and conversion over mere numbers.

WE BOTH TRIED VERY HARD TO COMPROMISE, AND TO HUMBLY EXPLAIN OUR SITUATIONS.

My investigations went a lot like Janet's: long, slow, and rocky. I hadn't attended LDS church activities very often for the last several years leading to my wife's betrayals and ultimatums, because I was trying desperately to sacrifice everything I could to try to make my marriage work. I was also really hoping that me building us a new larger nicer home, along with more intense attendance of Catholic services and school activities (my wife and children are all Catholic baptized and educated) might ease the general LDS opposition and negativity I kept encountering amongst my friends, associates, and even my own relatives.

STRUGGLING THROUGH IT TOGETHER.

Again, I didn't know Janet then, but she knew some things about me through friends at church. Janet's divorce had been finalized a couple years earlier. Now, she and her teen daughters finally were able to attend LDS church regularly, after so many years of a marriage so severely stressed because of those negative reactions to her investigations mentioned earlier. Especially the *extra* fatal input from her parents which had seemed to doom it from the very start (mentioned briefly back in Chapter 2)...

Vera and Don had gone to John fairly early in Janet's LDS investigations (but after they now had two baby daughters born within nineteen months of each other), and strongly encouraged him to divorce her, and assured him that they would do everything needed to legally get full custody of the grandbabies away from her, and for him. Vera was so very sure she was right and would win with this stratagem, that she immediately boasted tauntingly about it to Janet, who didn't doubt her one bit, but had absolutely nobody to turn to except God. So, she patiently but very faithfully hoped and prayed harder than ever for more time and patience.

John has never cared much about or attended any church, at least not in his adult life. But, he quickly realized enough about the intensity of Christian opposition to the "non-Christian LDS cult" that he agreed to consider the divorce and custody threat, confirming it to Janet. He waited many years to act on any divorce, but he forcefully mocked and angrily scoffed at Janet about "the F-#ing Mormons" thousands of times (always when they were alone, out of hearing of others). This was pretty much any and every time he felt any anger or wanted to punish her by "twisting the knife already stuck in her back" about it by her own parents.

This early back stabbing encounter with Janet's own parents had clearly added a more bold and snobbish level of cruelty and "pushy-ness" to John's constant need to belittle Janet, which traced back into the very roots of their personal courtship together. After all, if her own parents encouraged it, who else was ever going to defend her, or to stop his cruel taunting? What's the matter, Can't take a joke? And, apparently many other people were already rewarding him with desirable status, and plenty of pity and sympathy for it, also.

My eventual eighteen year marriage was similarly stressed by my investigation of the Church of Jesus Christ of Latter-day Saints, whose young missionaries had randomly knocked on the door of our little house one extremely cold winter evening in St.Paul, Minnesota, while my wife happened to be away. I was raised as an evangelical Lutheran. My family, friends, and associates were mostly kind, lovely people. But, the overall reactions from them about the supposed "cult problem" were consistently negative, although diverse in emotional intensity ranging from voiced statements of my foolishness, to anger, quiet sadness, confusion, lots of very subtle behind the back mocking to blatant in-your-face mocking, and even a fair amount of enraged scoffing.

EXAGGERATED FEARS AND INTIMIDATIONS

All of these reactions seriously scared and intimidated my wife, and repeatedly "submarined" any chance I had to re-establish or maintain any kind of normal marriage relationship. What kind of early group-association or investigation could possibly get you treated this badly? Especially by your own family and closest friends? Please try to understand how intimidating and scary this popular opposition can (and has) become for millions of innocent investigators and their families.

Thus, I too delayed any direct worship with the LDS after my first contacts with them, for over five years. Even then, I kept myself far from any full fellowship or culturalization of the sort the anti-cult publishers, ministries, and movements so shockingly scare and warn about. But, very much like Janet, I felt a strong prompting to find out the truth (especially since others were so pushy, and so wrong in their opposition). Thus, I too quietly started and continued a long, hard, serious investigation, mostly quietly on my own, mostly despite an unrelenting and irrational opposition.

Yes, both Janet and I have often delayed, hid from, ran away, compromised, or sacrificed any cultural connections we had from those contacts, but our families (feeling somehow so threatened) kept subtly punishing us as much or more anyway. If you can fully understand why this keeps happening so often, please let us and everyone know.

None of our children were taught or brought up LDS as younger children. Some have somewhat embraced it as adults, but all of them have very strong (some quite bitter) individual opinions about religion in general, especially because of the negativity and turmoil they saw about it their entire lives, and especially during their childhoods.

Note: Why so much pushy negativity? Why for so long? We were mostly merely investigating. We were never fully active, or fully culturalized. We were extremely vulnerable. It just doesn't make any sense. Yet, neither does anti-Semitism; whose foremost experts find it isn't even religious; it's mostly founded in exaggerated fears, jealousy, and envy of unfair Jewish education, talents, success, affluence, and supposed evil, anti-Jewish conspiracy theories of exaggerated hidden powers or evils.

Most fair-minded Americans are appalled and curious enough about this biggoted anti-Semitism that they try to study and understand as many different aspects about it as they can. The same is now happening slowly over this biggoted anti-Mormonism which has so obviously exaggerated and overplayed its hand to scare innocent investigators for so long and gotten away with it. And, without even much fair careful study or bystander-fairness offered, especially right here in the heart of America's proud Bible-belt.

LONG-STANDING WITNESSES, DESPITE THESE MANY WOUNDINGS.

But, despite this popular opposition (and probably largely because of it), Janet and I both had intensely researched, pondered, prayed, and sought the best answers possible from both sides, for ourselves (we certainly never intended to decide this for any other people, including our most precious children). And, we both had received a continuing series of incredible personal religious experiences** (far too precious and sacred for me to fully explain here).

> **Please ponder the quiet spiritual power and "light" provided to both Janet and me, and quietly search within your own heart to feel and find that same inner source of comforting peace and genuine courage to pick yourself up and move forward again. Janet and I both now believe that this still, small inner voice is a key answer to how we (especially Janet) survived so much, for so long. This book will revisit and explore this aspect of quiet spiritual power and light within each of us, in several later chapters.**

We each learned with continuingly full conviction that this was the story and pathway God desired for us (not necessarily for anybody else). We knew it, and we knew that God knew that we knew it. Thus, we dared not deny such continuing, profound, and powerful spiritual witnesses, which we were both absolutely and individually sure came from an all loving and all powerful God.

> NOTE: *Please understand that I don't expect, or even want you, or anybody else to be unduly influenced by our personal research conclusions or convictions. Such a pathway and convictions are not for everybody, and surely not for cowards, popularity seekers, or sympathy seekers. Many will evidently always consider such convictions the foolish "tricked beliefs" as caught or snared by that ingenious evil LDS-cult.*
>
> But, *Janet and I are both smart, educated, and well-read. We each took many long years of intense study to arrive there. We suffered and sacrificed greatly. We gained nothing and lost most everything*

every step of the way. We tried running from it and quitting for years, but our families and friends subtly punished us anyway. For some hidden reasons, mostly unintelligible to us then and now, they just couldn't let go of it, yet they insisted that we were to blame, because as they saw it, we *just wouldn't let go of it.*

So please, ponder your own unbiased outside opinions and perspectives here. Janet and I had repeatedly sacrificed everything for these innocent investigative answers and conclusions. Whereas, everybody around us during those critical times rigidly insisted on siding with the popular opposition, without the slightest compromise or fair, respectful consideration of our personal rights, feelings, or the resulting damage to us and to our precious young children.

Janet and I were both raised evangelical Lutherans, and we will always cherish those upbringings. We both also had lots of good exposures to good Catholics, Evangelicals, charismatic Pentecostals, and other churches and religions including Judaism, Hinduism, Buddhism, and Islam. And, we will always respect and admire most of those individuals and groups. In the many years since our childhood we have continued to worship with, and participate in many multi-denominational Bible studies and prayer groups.

We have been tested, and selected for multiple "auditioned" choir groups, all of which focused on non-denominational sacred religious music, and have performed (including a few solos) at many big Lutheran and Catholic churches. After all of our intense investigations, we have never found a need to give up or betray any of the most cherished Lutheran or Christian beliefs (at least not from our perspectives) that we had ever gained, whatsoever.

DEROGATORY LABELS

Nevertheless, our innocent LDS investigations stressed each of our marriages to the breaking point and repeatedly put us into impossible positions kind of like "half-breed refugees". I again apologize for using such a derogatory term as "half-breed", but I can't think of any other way to describe it.

We weren't really "Mormons". (In this lifetime, we can never possibly be the fully culturalized, stereotypical happy Mormon parents and family that the anti-cult ministries so harshly warn of), but yet we were very often singled out by those looking to mock and scoff at the supposed "non-Christian cult". Why do you suppose that kept happening? Why, even now, after over 45-years does it seem to never fully stop?

We were extremely easy and convenient targets, because our own families and spouses seemed to want us to be singled out, punished, or forcefully stopped from any further investigations if possible. So, they all seemed to believe that their negativity (whether subtle or blatant) was doing us a favor (kind of like Don and Vera claiming their abusive parenting was doing Janet and Lynn a big favor).

Anyway, nobody around us was ever going to defend us, which surely isn't true of members who have strong positive family support networks around them. As John would so often sneer at Janet, "What's the matter? Can't take a joke?" Taunting her, that he had such solid backing but she had nobody on her side, not even her own parents.

Many of the pushy people, who I believe wouldn't dare personally confront or challenge any established Mormons with supportive families nearby, have often picked me (or Janet or Anna alone) for unknown reasons. Please let me know if you have any ideas or further evidence for such selections.

Janet and I were both frequent targets in every way and everywhere for subtle criticism from both sides, and all sides. We were very much like the "half-breeds" or the refugees who have suffered so much, with almost nobody around them to really protect or defend them, or even to try to listen, or to try to understand them fully. Half-breeds might have a few close family-members to comfort them from the unfair bigotry, but refugees are almost always severely separated from family.

I don't want to blame or judge or prosecute anybody involved in any of these negative reactions. Most of them are basically lovely people who simply could not possibly fully understand all of the complex history and dynamics behind the anti-Mormon bigotry that was born in frontier America 200 years ago, and then perpetuated within the important family and friends around us by popular anti-cult ministries and publishers.

MORMON STORIES AND STUDIES THAT CAN NO LONGER BE IGNORED OR DENIED.

Peer reviewed historical treatises, of the highest and most unbiased academic integrity, have since then carefully studied and compared thousands of documented eye witness accounts from those early days. Many of these studies have documented, and are still now documenting a cursed American legacy of hypocrisy, criminal property destruction, theft, mass murder, rape, castrations, lies, rumors, half-truths, and slander for which nobody was ever even arrested, let alone convicted (not before the twentieth century, anyway). American justice, fairness, and religious liberty still has quite a ways to go before it can fully answer and account for this dark history and legacy.

For instance, in 1838 Governor Boggs of Missouri issued an extermination order making it legal to murder and violently evict Mormons. During those 1838 actions, seventeen innocent LDS-people were quickly shot and murdered within a few minutes time at Haun's Mill, a settlement of 75-families; with every person (including many others of the surrounding settlers there that day) either killed, mutilated, wounded, sexually assaulted, burnt-out, and/or permanently evicted. Similar actions were taken against tens of thousands of LDS sympathizers across a wide swath of the state of Missouri, until not one devout Mormon dared to live there then and for many years after that period. In the 1970s that order still stood intact, until 1976 when then Missouri Governor Kit Bond finally got around to rescinding that hateful and immoral order.

Many of the top U.S. universities have more recently found a need to create growing curriculums (sometimes entire departments) on Mormon studies because of the vast amount of historical documents which have not yet been adequately and properly analyzed and the importance of these historical documents, considering the overall history and development of these United States of America. Especially the western U.S., where the LDS church and peoples have played such significant roles, that their overall history simply cannot be ignored anymore.

I now challenge at least one of these many Mormon-studies programs to study some of the sociological questions asked within our stories; Why are the most vulnerable investigators (like Janet or me) repeatedly picked on?, and Why seemingly and endlessly over such a long period of time, even when they tried to stop or stay away from it?, and Why is there no known program to effectively help encourage bystanders to report it, intervene to help stop it, or to even ease it or help mitigate the damages? I had no idea that the responses evoked by our stories, and by this book could possibly vary as widely as we are finding. I don't take credit for all of this, and I have yet to fully understand it myself, so please someone should study some of this, further.

I do want to point out that somebody close to our own families (particularly the more educated, well read, and paid professional teachers, counselors, lawyers, or especially the reverend religious ministers) should have noticed that it was extremely unfair, wrong, and hurtfully hypocritical and un-Christlike to exclusively isolate us, knowing some were targeting Janet, me, or any other vulnerable investigators like us, with so much pushy and snobbish negativity. We both had innocent little children that were caught in the middle of those impossible situations, and those now grown children still suffer today because of those unfair stresses and injustices.

Something is very wrong in our communities, families, and nation today, that quietly allows such pushy and unethical anti-cult ministries, demonizing and labeling innocent investigators like us in such cruel and dehumanizing ways, and then blames and shames such investigators for being willing victims and fools of their own serious struggles, that the pushy followers of those ministries obviously helped create and then kept piling onto. (See Part 5, Chapter 12 for more of our struggles and stories about accusations that we actually had some strange "martyr-complex" and were somehow intentionally and selfishly seeking attention, sympathy, or pity from it all.)

It's now been over forty five years since Janet and I first started our individual investigations, and twenty seven years since we were married. Thus, she has proven, many times, to be the most incredibly loyal person to me, as well as the most wise, kind, and understanding of my unique personal struggles that I have ever found in my life. In fact, I sincerely believe I would be as good as dead, or disappeared into total insignificance (even more so than I already was, or am? - haha) had she not befriended me in some of my times of crises since those days.

IRONIC BENEFITS FROM INTOLERANCE, TOWARDS THE GENUINE.

I have briefly mentioned the terms "anti-Mormon" and "counter-cult ministries" several times. I have also mentioned the term "non-Christian cult" which is a frequently used term these ministries and others have hammered on referring to the mainline Church of Jesus Christ of Latter-day Saints for at least seventy years, though vehement opposition to Mormons can now be traced back 200 years. Each of these terms are subjects of enormous amounts of issues, attention, studies, and publications, and I cannot begin to cover even a small portion.

I would encourage you to search these issues yourself, go to online search engines, encyclopedias and religious portals. And please at least try to get a fair and balanced understanding from both sides of these various issues.

In that vein, I would always highly recommend using the young full-time LDS-missionaries, for at least part of your search. They serve innocently and without any guile towards or against anyone's faith or viewpoints. They can usually meet with you (in-person, by phone / texts, or online) almost anywhere or anytime at your convenience.

They can give you a very quick, but powerful observation about what ordinary LDS-people and families are actually like. And, of course they can speed your understandings about some of the different and odd, or strange-sounding aspects of the religion and culture.

It's been said, if the Church wasn't "true" these 18-year old missionaries would have surely wrecked it long ago. What other significant organizations have ever put thousands of ordinary 18-year old boys as their spokesmen, not just symbolically, but literally going into every city and neighborhood, un-chaperoned, door-to-door amidst massive rejection and significant numbers of pushy scoffers, and a long proven history of violence and murder -- especially against the most innocent adherents of their Church?

> Note: Historically, the mainline Church of Jesus Christ of Latter-day Saints has always somehow benefitted one way or another from such opposition --big surprise!!-- (I'm meaning

> THE-Church, but clearly not each persecuted investigator like Janet or me). When it caused people to leave, they were the weakest "saints" anyway. When it scares weak investigators off, they would have never lasted, anyway. Growing too fast, too easily, dilutes the overall member strength and quality of conversion. Embracing or harboring hypocrites or cynics within the church damages others, so better if opposition makes it uncomfortable, so they just leave. And, all free publicity is good in the long-run, even the endless and exaggerated negative publicity provided by this popular opposition.

LDS leaders rarely comment on any specific opposition. They will caution me, and prefer that I do likewise. I understand and agree with that wise-counsel. In fact, both Janet and I have patiently and quietly refrained from mentioning this for these forty five years. Most people around us know very little of this, and nobody has heard it all, until now.

Since we are finally telling and writing more of the story, I feel I need to mention a few details of the effects and issues of the intolerant popular opposition. Specifically, how it cruelly stressed and hurt us and our children, at and during our most vulnerable times and places. And also, how it shamed and made fools of our families and friends, by scaring, intimidating, or enticing them to join the mocking, or to just pretend and look the other way.

> NOTE: In some of my comments about the popular opposition and anti-cult or counter-cult ministries, it may seem to you like I am unfairly "bashing" them, or the veracity of their ideologies. I'm very sorry if it seems like that to you. I am merely telling our personal stories as fairly and as completely as I can. But, I can understand how it might be seen as "bashing".

We live in a day when political and religious groups regularly "bash" each other's positions and intentions. Throughout this book I have repeatedly encouraged more kindness and careful, respectful listening to each other, maybe even finding areas for compromise.

Please forgive me, and please form your own unbiased and fair opinions about these oppositions and ministries. I have encouraged all to not take offense. So, as I tell of our injuries from these oppositions, please understand that I intend to not be offended, rather to be more open to mending such injuries. Kindness is free, always kill'em with kindness.

Please understand that our long-suffering patience and perseverance is all we have ever had on our side during these long 45-years of our innocent investigations. I have never had much for earthly power or support in any of these things. Thus, I obviously have had absolutely no power to "bash" anybody about it, thus no intentions there either. We are finally telling and advocating for our own personal perspectives and sides in these stories, because nobody else ever has or ever will.

PROTECTING AND FORGIVING EACH OTHER.

It's never a mistake to have loved someone... Or, to have loved and hoped for better circumstances in one's life enough to have stayed, and sacrificed, even to the point of long-suffering damages. In this, we do not regret our previous marriages, nor the difficulties we lived through within those marriages. We both repeatedly chose to stay; and we worked very hard and sacrificed everything we possibly could for those marriages. We mostly didn't even complain when our own families and friends around us were making it virtually impossible to make those marriages work.

I sincerely do not want to unfairly criticize Janet's first husband, John. He is the beloved biological father to my two step-daughters, in that he has always been very stable and generous, especially to his legal and financial obligations. He had a very successful and stable career with a highly respected industrial corporation.

Of course he never hit Janet or the girls, nor did he ever verbally belittle his beloved daughters like he did to Janet. In fact, apparently he wasn't even aware of most of Janet's childhood abuse, because whenever Janet tried to bring up such issues or events, he refused to listen, and was simply unable (or unwilling) to believe any of it.

Janet and I both believe that John, and also my ex-wife and family (except for a few), were simply not capable of standing up to the popular and powerful opposition and all of the very unpopular complex history, exaggerated theories of evil or conspiracy, and half-truths, as well as the dynamics behind the anti-Mormon bigotry that still seems to exist around us to this very day.

Many very kind and caring Mormons tried to gently reach out to our spouses and children during those tense years before our divorces, to try to help ease the tension. We will forever appreciate the love and kindness of those courageous people.

However, in each case, it seemed to somehow always make it worse for us, within our families and especially with our very unhappy spouses. The dynamics in those situations seemed impossibly complex. I wish so much that I could provide some advice or solutions for anybody else in similar situations. I just cannot, because in our cases, everything seemed to always get worse in those regards, for some apparently very well hidden and covered reasons.

After Janet and I were married, and especially after we had to move to North Carolina then New York, we got to experience many places where we showed up for LDS-Sunday worship knowing absolutely nobody. Because I frequently traveled, or conducted new job-searches, these opportunities were multiplied. Many of the LDS-people who took the time to try to know us were fantastic, and often treated us better than we ever had or probably ever will be treated by our own families. We almost always found warm friendly greetings and treatment within minutes of walking through the doors of such new places and people.

Yes, once in a while someone would criticize or make wrong assumptions about Janet's health and medical issues, or about my lack of job or career security or employment benefits. Likewise about our lack of family unity, or previous marriage failures. But, we both had experienced far worse during our years alone, and with our closest family and associates intentionally betraying us (supposedly for our own good). Besides, we were on a journey or quest for genuine discipleship in Christ (to follow His pathways). So, it didn't really matter if we got mistreated. Certainly He, and His chief Apostles had been mistreated far more and far worse than we ever had, or would ever be.

Janet and I do not expect or want anything from anybody, as a result of publishing these stories. We merely hope that these stories have some value in helping each of us understand the hidden and denied irony within these struggles better. Perhaps we might even better understand the pathetic and unfortunate irony of the present struggles and lack of harmony within our nation, our homes, our marriages, our families, our churches, our schools, and our communities.

SOUL MATES

Long before I ever met Janet, I was working on writing some of my feelings and explanations to my family, hoping desperately that I could find something that might help open up some level of understanding. Years before meeting Janet, I had given out several drafts of that writing, about fifty pages to a few different people, but got nothing back from anybody.

Nevertheless, I decided to show a copy to Janet anyway, not expecting much back from her either. However, the next time I bumped into her, she absolutely "gushed" about how much it meant to her to read these struggles and feelings in somebody else. She said she had very carefully read it over multiple times, and was writing a response, but wanted to be sure she didn't give too brief a response to such heartfelt feelings that had obviously been poured out with a great amount of thought and care.

She eventually gave me a very long response letter, which significantly included several dreams (see Appendix: Janet's Own Words), and almost any discussions between us to this very day have seemed to take off where those first writings and soul-to-soul responses left off, binding us as true and lasting soul mates. Our listening and discussing usually confirms how different we think. But also confirms how this makes us stronger and much more formidable in combining our stories and our lives.

Please consider how important these stories might be for others out there who have suffered similar mocking injustices and bullyings. How many are out there, deeply wounded and feeling like Janet? I don't know. But, remember Janet couldn't even fully tell this story herself, let alone write it. I guess I was somewhat the same, as was Lynn, and Anna too. We need to write and collect these important stories somehow, somewhere. Please help us write and tell these stories for those untold others out there, wounded and suffering in silence over it all. It's far too big, too pushy, too much for any one person to tackle alone.

PERPETUAL UNDERDOGS

For personal and private reasons, both Janet and I have often felt strong individual kinships with various vulnerable underdog individuals and groups. I will not now endeavor to define in detail what I think an underdog is. However, I will say that we surely did not expect, want, or choose to be vulnerable underdogs ourselves, at least not for such a long, and impossibly difficult journey into such. Most true underdogs don't either.

Although nobody from either of our immediate families of origin had any recent higher education or higher social status, that was clearly not true of our ex-spouses. Both sets of their parents were university educated, and both of their fathers were high ranking executives in multi-billion dollar corporations. Also, both of their parents' families (siblings, cousins, uncles) contained numerous doctors, lawyers, judges, university professors, mayors, reverend pastors-priests, and highly successful business managers.

Thus, the more each of our ex-spouses realized how very stained we were somehow becoming by these underdog complications, and the more they worried about their overall family's approval, status, or reactions, the more they each seemed to desire being rid of us. They clearly did not want to risk the terrible disapproval possibilities within their own families and circles of being stained by any permanent associations with such perpetual underdogs, as Janet and I were both somehow clearly becoming.

I believe that these underdog stigmas and struggles were never just some simple coincidences randomly piling higher and higher upon both Janet and me. I have felt strongly for a long time that they were *much* bigger than that. That they were intentionally stigmatizing messages always meant, not just for us, but for gaslighting many others to learn from, as well, through powerful denials and cruel intimidation.

These negative stigmas will probably continue to pile up, until people can no longer ignore them or pretend that they just didn't exist or have any great importance or harm to anyone. That is why I have taken so much time and effort to try to tell these stories, in some kind of indisputable and meaningful way. And that is why I chose the theme: "Neither victims, Nor fools. Not ever!"

HOW DARE I CONFRONT SUCH POWERFUL AND POPULAR OPPOSITION AS UNETHICAL GASLIGHTING?

This chapter has provided huge clues and answers to how I, of all people, dared to seek and write about Part 2, Chapters 4, 5 of this book: ***My Quests: Fixing "Genuine Courage and Unity"***. My investigations and opinions here describe how I came to believe that the full potential of our American Dreams are threatened by the serious lack of American unity we are now experiencing, even witnessing such divisive disharmony increasing and threatening a possible second U.S. Civil War. I did not previously discuss it then, but I also believe that a similar divisive disharmony is now severely threatening the potential for good from the overall Christian movement, and even the full potential and understanding of the Biblical scriptures.

Janet and I both believe this overall Christian movement and its Biblical scriptures still hold the keys to finding and rescuing the full potential of our beloved American Dream. But, we believe that both the Bible & the Movement themselves need to be rescued from the diluted-down disunity and the divisive disharmony that they are currently stuck in.

We both believe that the U.S. founding fathers and founding documents were inspired by God and by the wisdom and divine truths, ethics, and morals found within the Holy Bible. Thus, we believe that the Holy Bible is actually a foundational document of ethics and morals for America and for the entire world, and that nobody can or should consider themselves adequately or fully educated without a reasonable understanding of those aspects within that Holy Bible.

BETRAYALS BY IMPORTANT LOCAL STATUS FIGURES POSING AS SPIRITUAL AUTHORITIES.

For example, early in Janet's LDS investigations, Janet's parents brought the Lutheran pastor, who for three years had significantly taught, led, and prepped Janet for her confirmation as a teenager, to boldly stop or talk her out of her investigations. By then, Janet had spent hundreds of intensely sincere hours investigating every aspect, to genuinely understand and get to the bottom of the controversy, including every exaggerated theory and half truth found throughout the anti-cult ministries and literature.

This pastor had also significantly instructed and evaluated Janet's adolescent faith and knowledge, signed her confirmation certificates, and did the ritual "laying on of hands" as "one ordained with the Spirit and authority". However, he had never even met a Mormon and proceeded to spend over an hour summarizing some of the weakest and most shallow points made from that anti-cult literature (per Janet's investigations).

He then proceeded to insultingly refuse to even listen to Janet's humble attempts to provide any humble or brief answers, or gentle explanation of her findings and views, as she now had a university degree and had obviously read and tested these issues far more than he had. Evidently, he came armed with these snobbish false presumptions gained mostly from his earthly status as Lutheran pastor, his degree'd seminary education, and his very shallow and quick skim of the anti-cult ministry's literature.

Janet was appalled that he did not even acknowledge any of his previous personal experiences with her, which was over three years of confirmation prep, or demonstrate any kind of genuine personal inspiration from knowing her, or supposedly being ordained with divine authority from the genuine Holy Spirit (as compared to the unmistakable Spirit, always brought by the much more humble and young nineteen year old LDS missionaries).

Of course Janet didn't argue or protest. Like always, she put these disappointments quietly away in her heart, and patiently waited for a day when truth and love might more fairly come forth.

I believe it is eminently ironic that my parents did the same to me, bringing the Lutheran pastor who had instructed and evaluated me through all three years of confirmation prep to boldly talk me out of it, and that he embarrassingly disqualified himself by acting in the same shallow, narrow minded, insulting, and prejudiced way towards me, as Janet's pastor did towards her.

By the way, Janet's pastor had also performed her first marriage ceremony to John only a few years before, and my pastor had married all four of my sisters, and had my father serving as deacon and church board member, including several years as president of that board during his pastorship.

> Note: Janet and I do not hold any kind of grudges or disrespect of Lutherans or their pastors, especially these two good pastors in particular. In fact, we both fondly appreciate and remember the many good things within our upbringing and experiences there. I am simply citing several examples where the shamelessly biased and divisive literature produced by those snobbish unethical and un-Christlike anti-cult ministries has hurt, divided, and embarrassed the entire Christian movement. Especially since those examples turned into over forty years of betrayed influence over our families and friends. Not quite the level of betrayal as Vera's enticement of John to divorce and steal custody of Janet's baby-girls, which then emboldened John's abusive mistreatment (Vera and Don went to John soon after the pastor failed with Janet).

Yet, because my pastor had such influence over my family for over twenty years, the betrayal was slightly similar for me. Most of my sisters, nieces, nephews, and cousins have long since left the Lutheran church, while I maintain excellent relationships with many congregants and pastors of local Lutheran churches near me (the towns and churches around me are mostly Lutheran), including connections to students and faculty at Luther College, only about thirty miles away. For several years I have been meeting every Monday morning, at least before Covid troubles, in a men's breakfast discussion group, including many local Lutheran leaders.

CHAPTER 8

STRUGGLES MAKE US STRONGER

EVEN THE UNFAIR AND FALSE PRESUMPTIONS

INVISIBLE STRESS DISORDERS: A QUICK LESSON ON PTSD.

Post traumatic stress disorder (PTSD) has now been extensively studied, and proven very real for soldiers exposed to too much violent stresses from war. Even though the evidence was overwhelming from most wars going back at least two hundred years, such "proof" was long in coming because the damages of PTSD are mostly unseen, and hard to measure. Not surprisingly, PTSD has now also been proven real for people, like Janet, who were exposed to too much violent stresses from childhood abuse. PTSD causes overactive adrenaline response, and other damages to normal stress hormones, thyroid, and metabolism. Eventually, it often causes a wide variety of auto-immune and auto-inflamatory disorders. Conditions in which the human immune system abnormally attacks healthy human tissues within the body, and which tend to come and go in strange flare ups of pairs or multiples.

Janet has often had symptoms and flare ups from several of these auto-immune and auto-inflamatory disorders from eczema outbreaks on her skin, to periodic serious episodes of hypothyroid, asthma, Crohns, ulcerative colitis, mouth sores, fibromyalgia, arthritis, and chronic fatigue syndrome. She considers herself lucky that none of these have ever disabled her to any terrible degree, even though her history proves she could have been the poster child for the violent childhood stressors which are only recently proven to trigger them.

During the fourteen year period of distancing from Don and Vera, Janet slowly and miraculously started having fewer and fewer flare ups of these auto-immune disorders. But until then, she patiently suffered in silence and misunderstandings. We can see clearly now that she really needed that distance to reduce her stress levels, but also to reduce the flare ups of these auto-inflammatory disorders.

After the major corrective surgeries, for the congenital malformations, Janet's physician teams realized that an associated PTSD aspect existed, and thus prescribed many different combinations of medications. They tried to provide the best meds they could find to restore as much normal function as they could. Several of these meds would make her groggy, and could very likely become addictive.

When a new time-release opioid painkiller Oxycontin came out in about 1995, her physicians were absolutely thrilled, and assured Janet that these pills would make her less groggy, and much less addictive than the previous alternatives (Percocet or Vicodin), due to the time-release design of each pill. Janet has always meticulously followed the prescribed dosing for all of her pills, but still started to notice signs of unusual dependence on the new drug. She discussed it with physicians, and they were surprised, but took her off the "oxy", and designed different combos of other meds.

MENTAL AND EMOTIONAL DAMAGES.

So far, I have only mentioned the physiological disorders from PTSD. However, there is also a long list of serious mental and emotional disorders associated with such stress, whether resulting from intentional abuse or not. I will not try to cover all of these mental health disorders here, but if you or anyone you know is having these issues, please make sure they get some professional help. Don't just pretend like you do not know it's damaging, when the stresses are obviously becoming way too much for that person at that time.

Janet did an amazing job of preventing such stressors from hurting her daughters. I know she did a far better job of that than I was able to do for my children; I already mentioned the damaging stresses on Anna as a teenager while I was so far away working in North Carolina. I hope these stories and Janet's example and wisdom might help others like me, who are not well equipped to prevent stresses and struggles in our own lives from hurting our children.

Because denials and embarrassments about these issues are so common, many people refrain from seeking or getting help. Also, because these issues and oppositions are so poorly understood or even acknowledged, finding a therapist who has even a slight understanding of these dynamics can be impossible. Thus, getting marriage counseling can be even more damaging than before seeking any therapy at all. I believe I was deeply wounded as a result of counselors who thought surely they understood it all, but then never even asked or carefully listened to my side or ever really acknowledged the amount of people impossibly piling on against me.

EASY TARGETS FOR EVEN MORE FALSE AND TOXIC PRESUMPTIONS.

Many family and friends have been concerned, and evidently somewhat critical of Janet's large bag of diverse prescription meds. Some, who have almost zero knowledge of her complex medical history, have been quick to jump to unfair and inaccurate conclusions about Janet's supposed "hypochondriac-like" tendencies. For various reasons, some of them seem repeatedly driven to find and use one thing or another against Janet's case, as if it were their personal business and responsibility to do so.

I have no desire to even try to understand or explain all of the vast complexities or implications of all of these meds. But, I do know that Janet has managed all of it amazingly well for the past thirty years of my knowing her medical history, and several times has successfully requested the physicians reduce meds, dosages, and/or replace certain pills. I also know that it is very easy and likely for people to criticize this and to jump to wrong conclusions about it. So, when combined with the forty years of negative reactions to her LDS investigations, we often find a difficult toxic soup of false assumptions that Janet must navigate with some people.

BADGES OF HONOR AND TESTIMONY.

Janet has always struggled with feelings of shame about her many surgical and birthing-scars, chronic-pains, extensive prescriptions, and inflammatory disorders; as if these were partially or totally her own fault. Over the years, even many doctors and clinicians have jumped to wrong assumptions and conclusions, before later taking the extensive time and effort to get a more complete medical history. And of course, none of them have ever got the full story, as told here.

One especially gentle white-haired temple matron once sat quietly down next to a dear friend of Janet's, who had come to the temple pondering and feeling very similar shame and sadness about such serious birthing-scars and medical issues. After a while without any kind of introduction or background the woman kindly whispered, "You know Christ-Jesus fell down on His face and pleaded with Father to possibly reduce His pains and sufferings – His bitter-Cup. And yet His Exalted resurrected body now bears scars of those sufferings as Eternal badges of honor and testimony. ...And that can never be taken from Him." That lovely woman then quietly sat there a little while longer and sweetly stood and walked away. Janet's friend was never able to learn who the woman was, yet she will never forget the soft words and the sweet feelings of lasting comfort she felt that day.

After Janet and I met, many new stresses were piled on to Janet's PTSD struggles. She was repeatedly sternly scolded and warned about befriending me by LDS leaders, because (despite the tragic separation literally destroying me and everything I was trying to do and to be) I was still legally married.

Vera even tactically threatened Janet that she had already started and would surely gossip more forcefully to Don's mother and to John's family that we were more than friends, somehow immorally sleeping together before marriage (she and John were now legally divorced over two years). And we were never, ever without suspicious chaperones, mostly including our five children, ages ten to sixteen. Whereas, both of our ex-spouses began serious extra-marital romances almost immediately upon separation (before divorce papers), without any attempts or need for discretion or concerns about outside criticisms or gossip from our closest friends or families.

Janet had initially hoped very much that my family and friends would accept and love her normally. That they would appreciate her helping me recover from such devastatingly damaging years of opposition, on top of the marital separation and divorce tragedy and stress. After all, her family of origin was so dysfunctional and abusive, she really needed and wanted a better place for her and her children to be connected to.

HOW-TO SINK OR SWIM (SURVIVE) IN THE "SHARK TANK"

For reasons nobody in my family has ever explained, they all withdrew from me then, unfairly and cruelly giving my traitorous ex-wife far more moral support and encouragement (despite her serious betrayals) than they ever gave to me, even though she has always gotten abundant support from all directions, and all of our family and friends. She then got even increased sympathy and extra-courtesy support from dozens of her own family and friends, and I got almost nothing but subtle scorn from anybody on either side. It was like they were all hoping that I would become so totally destroyed by it all that they would never have to face the Mormon investigation embarrassments ever again, and that Janet could not possibly last, or ever be anyone of significance in the families and circles formerly connected to me, so there was absolutely no sense or reason to befriend her.

Even now, after over twenty seven years of my marriage to Janet (we were married three months after finalization of my divorce papers), we both feel very uncomfortably disappointed that most of my family and friends just can't seem to fully accept her, and still seem to pretend she doesn't exist, or that she doesn't or shouldn't matter much to anybody within my family's events and relationships. My sisters have mostly never visited any of the five different purchased homes where we have lived since our marriage (not including any of the rental apartments or extended-stay rooms). The few times they did stop by, were filled with excuses for not being able to stay more than a few minutes.

Surprisingly, my first wife's family were much more gracious to me then and now than my own family were, however very infrequently encountered. I still appreciate that very much, but since she wanted and needed her family (and apparently also all of my family and friends) much more than me, I discreetly kept any connections there very remote, so as not to hurt any support that she wanted, and needed from all of them, ever since then.

Our teenage children (three girls and two boys, all within about five years of birth spacing) disliked and objected to many of these situations, and took almost any way that they could find, to secretly act against us back then. Soon, an unpopular mid-life wedding, blended family events, teenage drivers, peer behaviors, high school graduations, and tough college support decisions all came rapidly in succession.

And, to top it off, soon after our marriage, I lost a twenty year senior position (and career path) and had incredibly hard difficulties boot-strapping my career back from that point, while Janet's PTSD made it close to impossible for her to produce any significant income, despite trying as much as she could. My job searching eventually took us to North Carolina for over five years and then to New York for three, before finding a job back in Minnesota again.

In my case, almost all separated or divorced fathers in today's world are eventually presumed to be "dead beats" in some way or the other, especially if they have to give up or lose primary custody of their children. In an LDS world, where family is everybody's highest goal and responsibility, men are sometimes especially stigmatized by divorce and loss of primary custody. So, combining those unfair presumptions with the forty years of negative reactions to my LDS investigations, with almost nobody except Janet effectively trying to see my side after the hurtful and damaging divorce, and then add in the very fragmented professional engineering career (with many years of short-term contracting/consulting jobs, most often with zero fringe benefits within the employment package) that I had to deal with, and we often find another toxic soup of false assumptions that I have had to navigate as well.

Even today, after more than forty years of struggling against these diverse false assumptions, and the continued tendency of many people to keep finding some sort of avoidance or negativity towards one or both of us, we are still fighting a continuous uphill battle. Our own children often still find it easier to just accept and even side with these false assumptions, rather than attempt to stand up to so much popular opposition.

Pertaining to the biggest false assumption of them all: that our continued LDS investigations made us non-Christian "cultists". We now proclaim more assuredly than ever before, we vehemently insist (from forty five years of intensely tested experience) that we have never betrayed or given up any of our most cherished Christian beliefs, hopes, or covenants (at least not from our carefully and deeply studied perspectives). In fact, this book is a sure testament that our faith in the Holy Bible, prayers, and personal revelations from the Holy Spirit has actually grown rather than diminished.

I am an old, worn out engineer-scientist. I could never have written this book without lots of help and inspiration from God, or without help from Janet's gifted knowledge and relationship with God.

Of course, in the long run, virtually everyone closely related to us or otherwise concerned for us will eventually be hurt and damaged increasingly more, by the kind of unfair and unhealthy disharmony described here within so many close family relationships, if somebody does not step up. We've long hoped and prayed that things might get better, but it seems it might never happen now.

This situation badly needs a hero (or maybe a book?) to eventually help people understand better so that more of us can begin to heal and repair some of these impending damages, before they get too much worse. In that regard, I am sorry it has taken me so long to tell the hidden facts and feelings behind this story.

RISK BENEFITS, TENDER MERCIES, AND BLESSINGS.

So, why would anybody like Janet or me, let alone both of us together, bother to risk or maintain any kind of LDS investigation in the midst of such powerful, damaging, and popular opposition for this long? Or better yet, how could we possibly find enough time, energy, and other resources given the enormous stigma and false assumptions that kept cursing us all these years?

Obviously, our stories contain many complicated dynamics related to these questions, and something very positive must have been happening to justify these risks. But, fully answering or explaining all of these dynamics in our personal cases is not entirely what this book is about, so you'll each have to ponder and judge most of those things for yourself. If my persistence in writing this book, resurrecting my career, and creating a new life from the ashes of divorce and bigotry are not enough, I think I have described quite a bit about the very unusual and special "odd couple" bond that Janet and I have found together, with God guiding us.

As described earlier, I asked Janet why she thought God had let so much adversity fall on her and Lynn? She said near the end of her marriage, especially given her long struggles and the popular LDS-opposition, she prayed and even screamed at God reminding Him of the many great promises in the scriptures. Finally, after hours of ranting and sobbing (off and on for several weeks), a profoundly peaceful prompting came, and she prayed that she was willing to take any suffering if it would soften John's heart. Only a few weeks went by before she was scheduled for the second UTI corrective surgery to her bladder and kidneys.

I originally had included the entire story of the two priesthood blessings here, which I mostly moved up to Chapter 2 for earlier effect. These blessings were and still are very significant examples. And, there have been thousands of other significant spiritual experiences. Many which are just too precious, private, and sacred to include here now. Nevertheless, I will include a shortened summary of these two previously mentioned blessings (partial repeat) next, because they are so critical to understanding the next several sections, and because they are linked to our LDS-investigations which hadn't yet been mentioned or revealed in Chapter 2. So, to fully understand the story around this, please skim over these repeated blessings again.

1st blessing: "You will experience no pain. And, if you do feel pain you should remind Heavenly Father of this blessing, and insist that He honor it." And then he said, "Your husband and you will then grow together, first spiritually, then mentally, and finally physically."

As previously discussed, the man voicing the blessing was not a physician. He was the husband of a friend who loved Janet very much, so Janet thought to herself, "He has no idea what he is saying and must want very much for me to have that blessing", but she knew the pain part would be completely and utterly impossible.

2nd blessing: This second blessing came about a year later and was from the same man that had given her the earlier blessing. It included the words, "...something is about to be revealed that will require all of your strength and faith to overcome." Some friends wondered if it might be the impending divorce, but Janet, feeling a still small spiritual whisper in her heart and mind, said, "No, it's another health problem of some kind." Soon after that, her arm stopped working, and the fourteen inch syrinx spinal tumor, which had been there since her birth, was revealed after being hidden for so long.

After the two major spine and brain surgeries and recoveries, Janet finally agreed with John to finalize the divorce. John hated that these terrible surgeries and hospital recoveries had embarrassingly revealed some of his serious selfishness and failings as a husband, even to those who heartily sided with him about the Mormon difficulties. And, so they finally went ahead with the divorce papers.

I came along about two years after that, as an extremely vulnerable and emotional wreck, and Janet was soon to be again reminded of the strangely worded blessing, "Your husband and you will then grow together, first spiritually, then mentally, and finally physically."

I've now mentioned several times that I think that it is very significant, that we are an "*odd couple*" in many different ways, and during this time period particularly, we were both very surprised by the incredible strangeness of events occurring, as if God was almost pushing us towards each other, spiritually and mentally, for some unknown reasons, that we both felt quite surprised and more than a bit uncomfortable about, because He was also severely testing us physically and emotionally.

Janet, of course, knew that I mostly needed spiritual and mental encouragement after the endless and impossible negative reactions by my wife, friends, and family. And, of course she and I both knew the terrible risks and perils of any hint of romance or physical attraction to each other. But, she also recognized better than anybody else around me how deeply and seriously hurt, damaged, and vulnerable I was, and for some reason she was willing to risk it and/or even suffer it for my sake.

I remember her taking enormous time and effort to try to give me a different "reflection" of myself than the ones I had been getting back from my wife and family for so long. When I objected, and refused to accept her new perspectives, she merely found other wisdom and evidence until she finally began to turn my poor and almost destroyed self images around.

As I remember back on her gentle encouraging words and efforts on my behalf then, I am repeatedly amazed at how she was somehow able to understand aspects about myself that I am still trying to figure out about me, even today.

THE HUGELY WORRISOME KING COBRA DREAM.

I have always felt a deeply ingrained fear of big snakes, and in boyhood I remember many dreams where I would wake in a sweat after some usually vague dream about snakes. One dream, though, came repeatedly, very clearly and with great detail. I was assigned a task to repair a zoo exhibit for a large female King Cobra snake. I strenuously objected due to my lifelong fear of snakes. But, I finally agreed to the task and was told the snake was currently deep underground healing from serious injuries. I completed most of the tasks without ever encountering the snake, but remember several dreams where the snake returns from underground partially healed and very edgy.

Weeks later, a dream came where I was required to enter the exhibit and carefully learn to allow the snakes to touch me, and for me to touch them in preparation for a traveling rail car exhibition tour. The exhibit included the offspring and grandchildren of the female parent snake, and all were very dangerous, including biting and spitting venom. The tour was important to provide understanding and healing anti-venom to the people amongst whom these types of snakes lived in the wild. These dreams reoccurred always with me waking in a sweat.

I had these dreams many long years before ever meeting Janet. But I've now come to realize (through several unusual and incredible promptings) that the snakes at least partially represent issues included in this book. To some degree, that Janet (and maybe my mother and sisters, or even my ex-wife and her various friends) was represented in that large female parent snake, and that the exhibit repair and the traveling rail tour are these stories, and this book, which have taken so many years of my personal risks, struggles, and effort to provide.

I also remember in various dreams that a close female advocate was there supporting me, but I never knew who exactly it was because she always seemed to stand beside me, but just enough behind me that I somehow could not fully recognize her. For years I assumed it would eventually somehow become clear that it was (and would be revealed to be) one of my sisters, my first wife, or maybe Anna. Now, I am quite certain that person must have always been Janet (then, now, and forever).

STRUGGLES HAPPEN TO EVERYONE; SO TRY TO HAVE THE BEST, HAPPY LIFE YOU CAN.

For the past three and a half years, Janet's ninety-one year old dad, who now has severe dementia, has lived in our home with us. The people of our little town, Lanesboro, MN, see us bring him to the community's senior dining program every day. Many are also very aware that we sacrificed and worked very hard to put an expensive addition on our home, so that he has his own self-contained apartment off our basement, with his own private entrance. Soon, we will need to hire a home health care nurse, but for now Janet and I provide his meals, laundry, cleaning, prescriptions, and chauffeuring. We also schedule his doctor, dentist, and barber, stock his fridge, and help with his mail, taxes, and finances. We try to help our community. With me training and serving as certified Emergency Medical Technician on our volunteer ambulance service (which during this 2020 Covid-19 pandemic, now needs me very much).

What they, or anybody else for that matter, don't know is that for five years before Don's moving here, Janet had nearly killed herself (as documented in her blood pressure, and other vital medical histories), driving back and forth (twenty hours round-trip) nearly a dozen times each year to Indiana, trying to help care for his needs. So many of which were becoming increasingly minor and pathetic. They can't possibly know how easy it is for Don to "push Janet's buttons" and trigger a PTSD-type reaction in her, deep inside, back to those terrible childhood days. Usually, Don isn't intending such, and isn't even aware he is doing it. Mostly, he is merely mimicking the same old negativity dialogs towards her, that he and Vera had maintained all of their lives together.

Anyway, despite these negative triggers, Janet somehow designed and planned out a major addition on our century-old plain American Foursquare house (probably originally a Sears mail order house-kit). Then, despite knowing almost nobody here and never having done so before, she managed to find the appropriate contractors, purchase the appropriate materials, and manage the entire project through to completion on top of all of her other worries, struggles and concerns (saying that was merely super functional is a gross understatement).

Again, it's important enough for me to repeat here; that Janet never did anything with the medical documentation for legal recourse mentioned earlier. She did however complete a wide variety of personal counseling and therapies. She sent several loving and heartfelt letters well before her mother died eight years ago. They were rejected with angry replies.

> *"Interestingly, they did not deny anything. In fact, Janet was very surprised that their replies actually affirmed much of what she wrote about. Yes, besides the hospital file of documented parental abuse; Janet now also has written letters affirming many of the most damaging childhood abuses, in their own handwriting."*

After Lynn's defiant enlistment into the Army, as soon as she heard Janet was investigating the LDS church she also decided to investigate. Since she was single, she was able to be baptized - over 15 years before Janet was able to. She got married and had a son, and proceeded to struggle financially the rest of her life. Since her parents continued to consider her a 'throw-away' they not only didn't help her, they significantly hurt her (both financially and emotionally) many times because of her vulnerability, and evidently because of her defiance.

As discussed earlier, "Janet has no desire to judge the overall intentions or reasons behind her parents' actions. Nor does she want to hurt or to denigrate them. We believe that these stories will help add examples and understanding for the rest of this book. And, we hope they also help someone out there who may have experienced some challenges or struggles related to abuse or zingers like them.

Janet always says that; the best response to negative criticisms and reactions is: to just have the very best and happiest life that you can possibly have, given your circumstances, and to doubt your doubts before doubting your faith. So, this book is our answer to that wise perspective.

We do not regret any of it, because it has all helped us to become stronger, and better people, than we would have or could have been, had we had things come more easily for us. This book is one huge evidence of God's help and assistance; without which I could never have persevered long enough to finish and promote this book. We have truly tested our faith and beliefs ourselves over a very long run of popular opposition, and proven the adage... Struggles make us stronger, so the best is yet to be."

> *"Rivers do not drink their own water; trees do not eat their own fruit; the sun does not shine on itself and flowers do not spread their fragrance for themselves. Living for others is a rule of nature. We are all born to help each other. No matter how difficult it is. . . . Life is good when you are happy; but much better when others are happy because of you."*
>
> —Pope Francis, also in Sūktiratnahāra (14th century, by Sūrya Kalingarāja).

CHAPTER 9

BETTER UNDERSTANDING THE POSITIVES AND NEGATIVES OF ZINGERS.

So far, the stories, ideas, and concerns expressed within this book have been most heavily influenced by negativity. Yet, my foremost intentions for this book have always been to create a positive overall outlook, including ideas to repair the negativity and divisions, because "...the *best* is yet to be."

Certainly, we live in a world and time of great negativity. But, I don't think that is entirely bad, or entirely new. Negativity has always played a huge role in the recorded histories of every culture and time. As repeated earlier; struggles make us stronger, so the *best* is yet to be. Likewise, powerful, direct, and popular oppositions and negativity, if not too overwhelming, can also make us stronger. In fact, many experts think that negative interactions have always had a significantly greater impact on human memories and on humanity in general than neutral or positive interactions. Such "negative effects" contribute to a significant and important "negativity bias" within every human culture.

In studies of self esteem, it has been shown that every negative criticism is likely to be remembered for years, but positive praise is often forgotten within minutes. Thus, It can take a thousand "attaboys" to erase one "You're as worthless as..."

Don and Vera always seemed to have a great faith in the power of negativity (negativity bias). In the short run, such negativity often does get powerful results. As parents, they proved both the ability to apply it and use it to the extreme, and also to effectively cover it and hide it when it might work against them.

They often hid behind their material assets and their status in the communities where they interacted and behind masks of faked positivity, such as good humor and pleasantries, which seemed easily within their grasp. They also creatively used the popular LDS opposition, and other negativity to divisively turn Janet's own husband and family against her, to suit their selfish purposes. Vera must have believed in the power of rewards as well, because she seemed to love dangling promises and possibilities of rewards (and prospective entitlements such as paid college, cars, loans, weddings, and support for grandchildren) in front of her daughters, and others.

However, clearly they believed in the power of negative punishment more, because per Janet and Lynn, whenever it came time to deliver on any of those dangled promises, Don always stepped in and provided an impossibly long list of excuses and reasons why they just could not in good conscience pay out the promised reward, citing vague "tax penalties" and such. Of course, they would have been very aware of "the carrot vs. the stick" metaphor for rewards and punishment, as many popular news journals and cartoons during their lifetimes depicted this metaphor.

A LASTING LEGACY OF SELF-SABOTAGE

Many political and social movements and leaders today, as well as those reaching back to ancient times have all seemed to understand how to selfishly and effectively use both negativity and positivity to their advantage. It is the rare leader or movement that is patient enough to use them for optimum goodness (or without stretching and diluting standards of ethics and morals).

To understand this more fully now, I will briefly revisit these points. As we stated earlier, *"the best leaders and zingers for change have always insisted on responsible, respectful non-violence, both in words, actions, ethics and morals, no matter how much longer it takes. Such leaders usually patiently try to go as positive as possible, with any negativity quickly and carefully followed up by some kind of respectful reassurance."*

Whereas, the most selfish and corrupt leaders and zingers have always sought the quickest, easiest pathways possible to social change (in words, tone, and in actions) no matter how disrespectful, negative, hurtful, angry, divisive, and extreme (almost always using the age old "*the end justifies the means*" rationale someway, somehow). And, sometimes (more covertly) using the situational ethics of "*almost anything is okay, as long as you don't get caught.*"

I have pondered and prayed about these aspects of leaders and zingers, many hours, and many times. I strongly believe that this rare aspect of virtuous patience is a very significant factor in comparing and judging the good, better, and best leaders from the worst.

For some reasons fully unknown to me, unrighteous and corrupt leaders almost always choose the quickest and easiest pathways to change. Those quick and easy pathways almost always include some kind of extreme forces of shame, negativity, or extreme positivity, to forcefully entice, or to dominate their followers, not allowing them the dignity and freedom of forming and choosing their own unimpeded personal opinions, or agency.

Such selfish leaders, groups, and movements are easily seen, and commonly found in U.S. culture today. They are so common it is rare to find anything but such selfish leaders and groups everywhere, in our governments, politics, businesses, communities, schools, churches, families, and even our marriages and homes.

- The rarely found good, better, and best leaders and groups who advocate more courageous-patience are often resented, mocked, and scoffed at, making such even more rare, and requiring even more rare courage to stand firm and stay clean from these strong negative snobbish tendencies all around us (to dilute our ethics and morals). But, it is not yet impossible to find pockets of such goodness. I encourage you to look and find these pockets of goodness around you. And, when you find them, by all means, don't be afraid. And, don't be so easily put off by the cowardly mockers and scoffers.
- This isn't the purpose of this book, and I never wanted to be the bearer of such bad news. But please, don't shoot the messenger.

THE PROBLEM OF EXTREME (TOXIC) POSITIVITY.

Of course, we've always had strong pockets of positivity in every age and culture of this world of ours, such as positive religious leaders and preachings, positive business sales & marketing people/campaigns, positive political people and slogans, and positive self-help and motivational speakers, books, and materials.

The trouble with these pockets of positivity is, they have always proven to be unusually susceptible to incursions of extreme scoundrels, scams, counterfeits, and confidence men. This can be notoriously and historically proven, as evidenced within almost every recorded culture since ancient times, particularly within the most prominent ancient religious cultures and scriptures, such as the Greeks, Romans, the Bible, Koran, and Dharmic records. No matter how much evidence and warnings about such leaders those ancient religious cultures kept falling into the same old materialistic and pride trappings.

Our Founding Fathers knew of this, thus they spent volumes of time discussing and creating a "balance of powers" into our U.S. Constitution, and an establishment clause into our Bill of Rights. Clearly they were very concerned about the abuses they saw by the alliances between government leaders and powerful religious and church leaders from the state churches of Europe.

Now, we can confirm their concerns. When observing similar "subtle bullying alliances" formed by the powerful modern elite "high priests" of academia, the sciences, celebrity entertainment, mass media, business sales & marketing, and even big labor unions and crime cartels. Such extreme corrupt alliances seem out of control, with little hope for much change. These modern alliances seem to spend and lobby incessantly to gain corrupt influence with our political and government leaders (and also with other covert and illegal, sometimes even criminal, business leader agreements, both national and global).

But, these corrupt alliances keep suffering endless divisive gridlock, and inefficiency. They are able to achieve hypocritically faked levels of unity and positivity, but they clearly will never be able to achieve the kind of lasting positive peace, unity, and results that they so confidently promise.

Ambitious and pushy populist leaders are not new, either. But today, we are seeing them much more than ever before. Millions of ordinary citizens are using social media sites and apps to build unusually large volumes or networks of followers, hits, likes, shares, and posts. Many of them are learning that they can cash in on these networks in a wide variety of ways. And so, temptation to use exaggerations, juicy rumors, extreme theories or speculations, conspiracies, or other shocking information, including lies, half-truths, and divisive insults, becomes strong.

Reality-tv shows, shock-jock talk shows, and some special interest and gossip blogs/ podcasts are other examples of those using and proving greedy tactics to rush the building and growing of their populist followings and influence, often taking advantage wherever possible of our culture's most vulnerable and spoiled people. These are people who, for various reasons, feel pathetically entitled, dependent, and/or addicted to materialistic hopes, dreams, or substances. Many of them are looking and hoping so fondly for a quick, free feeling or assurance of being "Saved" within their concept of Christian-salvation. Or maybe a "lottery ticket to easy street." They might actually spend much of their scarce money and time in casinos, or buying and checking tickets for big state-sanctioned lotteries, or falling for other get rich quick, or quick and easy something-for-nothing schemes.

THE EVER POPULAR LDS OPPOSITION.

The LDS negativity is a good example. Since it's been such a big part of our stories, I need to cover some basic aspects. However, I want to specifically stay away from any comprehensive point by point issues within this LDS negativity, because this is an enormous subject, with many very complex arguments on both sides. Hundreds of shelves of books and booklets have been published over the last 200 years, including thousands of volumes, and many more being written, and yet to be written about these points. In fact, the sheer volume of this popular opposition, and even more so of the quality and quantities of apologist defense responses, prove the immense importance of these points within the overall Christian movement and progressions.

A QUICK LESSON ABOUT THE NEGATIVITY ASSOCIATED WITH THE TERM: 'CULTS'.

The lovely people (even close family) who were involved in opposing our stories and our investigations felt strongly that they were doing everybody a favor. And, because the overwhelmingly popular opposition to all "cults" surely (without question in their minds) justified a reasonable level of negativity, I will address the broad generic and negative subject of such cults, since this popular opposition uses that term so often, and because it played such a big role in our personal stories.

During the 1970s, many new, large and active anti-cult groups and movements grew up around the world, and especially in the U.S. The U.S. already had several focused religious ministries and publishers, which had started about the 1950s, opposing supposed quasi-christian groups like Jehovah's Witness, Seventh-day Adventists, and LDS (Mormons) mostly on theologic, apostasy, and supposed heresy claims, and the perceived need to protect youth and other vulnerable people. Anti-cult groups multiplied and expanded greatly during the 1970s growth spurt in anti-cult groups, many of which were more secular and focused more on the secular "mind control," "brainwashing," and aggressive "proselytizing" approaches.

The late 1960s and early 1970s saw explosive growth in new religious groups and communes. Eastern religious and mindfulness ideas and techniques were being introduced widely amongst intellectual and college communities. Popular Rock'nRoll music and illegal drugs were new factors in attracting many younger people, as well as anti-establishment protest movements and ideologies.

There is no question that dangerous new religious leaders and groups exist today. Since the late 1960s, they began to multiply and grow even within the largest, most established churches, justifying a certain amount of reasonable concern and activities. In fact, major governments around the world began creating "danger watch" lists and reports on such dangerous sects, cults, and new religious movements, because of legitimate concerns surrounding them. Many of these leaders and groups, included terrible corruptions, comfortably hide within the major established religions and mainline churches. Take, for example, the many Islamic extremist and terror groups, though almost every major religion and mega-group has examples and leaders hiding, planning, and doing bad things usually hidden somewhere on the fringes.

There are related concerns among government and academic observers that some of the "anti-cult" groups were using these popular concerns to justify unethical activities themselves. They encourage and use the word "cult" with just as much prejudice and antagonism as the worst racial slurs or derogatory words for women and homosexuals, all for their own selfish gains. The term or label -- "cult" is clearly used to effectively demonize the group and its leaders and dehumanizes its members and children, especially recent converts or investigators who do not have any established support networks or backups around them.

Interestingly, the mainline Church of Jesus Christ of Latter-day Saints does not even show up on most of these "danger watch" government lists, whereas many fringe LDS, Pentacostal, Evangelical, and Catholic groups do show up, because of serious and proven concerns about their unethical practices and coverups of financial extortion, child abuse, and sexual abuse. Yet, these religious countercult ministries, and "anti-cult" groups seem to hypocritically ignore these popularly accepted linkages and other biased hypocrisies and complications within their connected leaders and movements.

At this time within all of the major established religions of the world, especially within Christianity, when so many divisive fractures are occurring and with so many bad actors showing up everywhere, especially among the most ambitious and successful leaders in the fastest growing mega-groups, we all need to ponder these danger watch lists. Clearly these serious concerns and investigations into unethical cults or sects and leaders need to expand to include the mainstream and established churches and institutions, especially including these anti-cult ministries, media, and publishers. Please ponder these things, and tell us your own stories and perspectives about them.

I do not want to focus on this subject alone. It is not the intention of this book, and many others are already addressing these concerns. However, I needed to include some since it is such a big part of our stories, and there have been few stories that have been able to tell such vivid and hurt filled details of this side, along with evidences and aspects of the dangers and effects on innocent people like us caught up in the middle of these popular oppositions and struggles.

Of course, Janet and I are not the only ones who have suffered such opposition. There have been millions of LDS converts over these forty five years of our investigations. Many had their spouses and children comfortably investigate and converted together with them, so they were not nearly as vulnerable. Many others were younger, so they were able to comfortably marry or assimilate into established LDS families, and communities.

As I said, we are not really looking for sympathy or anything from anybody, other than to tell our important stories here. But, since our stories provide detailed evidence of indisputable damages, maybe they can help someone understand it better. Maybe someone can someday put together some kind of petition, organization, or maybe even a class action suit against several of these most unethical and highly profitable anti-Mormon ministries and publishers. I believe we wouldn't hesitate to sign on, mostly to stop, or slow down such damaging bigotry from hurting future vulnerable families, children, and individuals.

OF MENTAL ILLNESS, MENTAL DISABILITY, OR OTHER MENTAL DISORDERS.

Everyone, at times in their lives, encounters stresses that are simply too much for them to function, or to handle effectively at that time. In fact, to some degree we get there every day, as fatigue and wake-time stresses pile up until we choose to go to bed for normal rest and recuperation.

When we get exposed, either by choice or by circumstance, to seriously excessive amounts of such stresses and struggles, we all sometimes have more serious mental or emotional meltdowns, breakdowns, or burnout. For instance, when such serious stress happens, one night of normal rest and recuperation is clearly not enough, and so these strains can accumulate and pile up, causing even greater problems.

- If this more serious mental or emotional stress happens repeatedly over a long period,
- If these struggles are magnified by other stresses, tragedies, or negative and dysfunctional behaviors of those around us,

- If we, or others around us choose maladaptive, addictive, and destructive behaviors to cope, such as:
    - Excessive TV or electronic game playing
    - Excessive day dreaming, worrying, or negative criticisms of self or others
    - Serious substance abuse or self medication with illegal drugs, alcohol, tobacco, coffee, or even fast food
    - Negative blaming, complaining, shaming, or destructive gossiping
    - Violent outbursts, verbal attacks, hitting or hurting others or themselves
- If any of the above becomes chronic, they can seriously damage our health, mentally and emotionally for sure, but also even physically if they are continued too long.

These more serious mental or emotional meltdowns, breakdowns, or burnouts usually make us more fragile to any other types of stresses and struggles around us, even the normal day to day struggles of everyday life.

COPING SKILLS AND STRATEGIES.

> Note: The next paragraph was included in Chapter-3, but is repeated (in short summary) here because of the relative importance to understanding this section; and coping with these stresses, especially given the added info (not yet mentioned in Chapter 3) about the chronic popular LDS opposition endured as described in this chapter.

In adulthood, Janet and Lynn both, at times, withdrew into maladaptive mental escapes of denial and fantasy daydreaming. Earlier I described how Janet's fantasies about suicide were helped and stopped by her habitual caring and worrying for her sister, as well as the "still small inner voice" that she had learned to quietly listen for and to trust. Somehow, these extra burdens of responsibility, care for Lynn and for her parent's harsh demands kept Janet from slipping further into any maladaptive behaviors. I believe they actually kept Janet trying different things, until she began stumbling across more healthy and functional approaches that I can recognize in her, even today. *For instance:*

- *Her ability to bravely admit and face fears, mistakes, limitations.*
- *To embrace vulnerabilities, and keep trying something else that might work.*
- *To find solace in humor, laughing, music, and great stories, literature (scriptures).*
- *To keep pondering (praying) and learning about the root causes, and to find genuine gratitude wherever possible.*
- *To believe and act as if true-change (repentance) is possible (that God helps).*
- *To patiently serve others, even when they don't acknowledge or appreciate it.*
- *To quietly, patiently, and courageously sacrifice, even suffer for the sake of others.*

Our modern culture keeps increasing these stresses, but then pretends they aren't serious, and often even tends to hide and deny them when they surface as behavioral dysfunction or illness. Too often they are hidden, denied, mishandled, mislabeled, and mistreated. Some of the blaming, shaming, medication alternatives, and institutionalizations can become tragic problems for such vulnerable people caught in such overwhelming stresses and sufferings.

Our stories reveal many years when Janet, Anna, and I were struggling through serious stresses like this. Anna hit that point as an exceptionally vulnerable teen, with her dad (me) far away in North Carolina. In Janet's case, her life story could easily make her the poster child for the various mental or emotional stresses and disorders that usually result from such childhood abuse, and she still has to work at healing and maintaining sanity from her past.

Please take a lesson from Janet's survival and courageous coping; You can move forward from even the worst situations. It won't be quick or easy. Rather, it takes genuine patience and courage, and it takes faith, understanding, and help from God and others.

In fact, our stories indicate intentional and collaborative piling-on and even gaslighting denials that there ever was any unusual pressures on each of us. I don't think anyone actually wanted us to lose sanity, but they felt fully justified in controlling the narrative, while denying and excluding our feelings or perspectives on these situations.

So again, after reading all of this; How do we 'kill' the Mocking Birds? Kindness is free, so you know what to do.

CHAPTER 10

MY ENGINEERING CAREER

EARLY EXPOSURES INTO EXTREME "US VS. THEM" POLITICS:

I retired from engineering in 2019. The last 15 years, working in Minnesota's medical device industry, were by far my best, most enjoyable years. I worked mostly as a Quality Assurance Engineer on development teams, completing process validation and verification studies on the manufacturing of a wide range of devices and components for implantable medical devices, from neurostimulators used for deep brain therapies to implantable heart pacemaker systems, and many precision surgical tools and kits for implanting them.

I loved that work, but the roundabout roads getting there included some very unstable scrambling. From a brief start in the steel and coal industries, to almost twenty years at a federal minerals research lab, and then ten years of frantic job searching and scrambling in between.

MINNESOTA "NICE"

I was born in Hibbing, Minnesota, where the great Bob Zimmerman (Dylan) grew up and graduated high school. A little like Bob (oh no), I have often been seen as an overly serious, sensitive, and thoughtful person or a daydreamer, concerned enough about irony, negativity, and verbal zingers to say and write something about it. He wrote songs with poetic lyrics; I am writing stories. He got strength and inspiration from experiencing anti-Semitism from those outside of his family and friends; I got strength and inspiration from experiencing anti-Mormonism from those within my own family and friends. Bob and I both know that such "struggles make us stronger, so the *best* is yet to be". Bob and I both enrolled and attended our freshman years in college at the University of Minnesota, Minneapolis campus (me in 1971, Bob in 1959). I finished, he didn't. He won a Nobel prize in literature. Me - not so much.

I was brought up as the middle child of five children. The only boy surrounded by four sisters in a mild mannered, loving Lutheran "Minnesota-nice" home. For some unknown reason, all of my life, I remember spending lots of time pondering and dreaming about the bigger questions and mysteries of life. Yes, I was a daydreamer, and I guess I still sometimes am.

I was spiritually minded, and I felt the peace and unity of the Spirit numerous times during religious worship services. I think I was a good boy, but I regret to say that as a teenager, I decided and made some bad choices. Mostly, I was merely trying to fit with a more popular crowd. I always felt bad about straying outside of parental expectations (though nothing serious or criminal), but knew that I would eventually seek to return myself to those feelings of spiritual peace and unity that I had experienced as a boy.

Having come from such a humble, unremarkable, sometimes even wayward background, how and why could I, of all people, dare to write about supposedly understanding such chronic, unsolvable worldwide problems, including suggestions for solving those problems such as:

- Neither victims, nor fools! About all underdogs and scapegoats, ever, and their struggles.
  - » About being gaslighted, trivialized, or marginalized, as willing "victims" or "fools" of one's own struggles.
- The historical and worldwide irony of verbal zingers; which provide clues to hidden intentions and objectives of popular leaders and groups.
  - » Especially at this "Alarming Apex" within the Information Age.

- Seeking a "Genuine Unity" for the entire world, especially at a time of such exaggerated divisiveness.
- Developing and maintaining a "Theory or Story of Everything" to help repair the American Dream.

Of course, finding Janet as my companion and soul mate has helped immensely. But even more than this, our mutual and fundamental faith in higher hopes, beliefs, sacred music and scriptures have created a shared sounding board for our highest ponderings and prayers for our families, for God, and for the inspirations and visions connected to the universally inspiring "American Dream."

UNIVERSITY IMPRESSIONS.

As a young, impressionable under-grad student at the University of Minnesota Minneapolis campus from 1971 to 1975, I witnessed and read about significant national political protests going on almost every day on my campus. Most were exaggerated and extreme anti-establishment protests about the Vietnam war, abortion issues, women's rights and reproductive rights issues, LGBT issues, racial-injustice, animal mistreatment, or environmental issues (very often against metals production and minerals mining, which was directly against my major field of studies - Minerals Engineering).

Of course, a few of the protests were against some of the extreme-liberal exaggerated-left positions. These were the more conservative pro-establishment positions; pro-life, anti-abortion, pro-gun-rights with much smaller protest-groups and much smaller followings.

The enrollment of the Minneapolis campus of the U of MN was huge and diverse during those years. Due to the "baby boomer" generation and vast numbers of commuter students from the thriving Twin Cities metro suburbs, it had well over 50,000 under-grads, plus huge numbers of graduate, extension, and exchange students, making it nearly the largest single university campus population in a single physical location in the world at that time, or any time since then.

The campus newspaper, the Minnesota Daily, published since 1900, is the largest student run and student written newspaper in the U.S. and winner of numerous prestigious awards, including best all around daily student newspaper in the country, several times. In 1971, the campus elected gay activist Jack Baker as student body president. Jack, a first year law student then (though I never met him), had recently married his same-sex partner, making them arguably the first legally married same-sex couple in the history of the United States. (Of course the full-legality of that early same-sex marriage is debatable and desputable.)

In the spring of 1972, my freshman year, the protests against Nixon's military mining of Hanoi harbor in North Vietnam blew up into major rioting, burning, destruction, and violence by and against the police sent in to put down the rioting. The police used dogs, tear gas, riot clubs, and helicopters spraying pepper fog, but the protests and riots kept going for eight days. The police failed to fully clear and control the rioters because the events attracted far too many people, mostly onlookers and "bystanders" curious to see what would happen when the police finally got more strict.

I was still a very impressionable eighteen year old, who had come from a small rural backwoods community and high school (Nashwauk-Keewatin High School) only about a hundred miles south of the Canadian-border. Many cars were turned over and burned, and many people and police were injured during those "eight days in May" riots. The membranes of my eyes, nose, and throat burned from tear gas and pepper fog multiple times as I walked through my college campus that week, and several times I thought I might even get caught in the chaos and maybe even get hit with a police riot club.

To say the least, I often felt very disturbed by the extreme intensity and negativity of these anti-establishment protests. And as I was later surrounded by many of the foremost faculty experts in minerals and mining, I eventually became more and more aware of how many exaggerated lies and half-truths these many various environmental protests used in their extremely negative propaganda-laced rants about mining and minerals production.

CAREER PROTESTERS IN THE LATE 1960S TO 1970S.

All of the biggest protest events on my campus were at least influenced by teams of career protesters who were paid out of massive funds raised by political fundraising. Many events were headlined by protest celebrities. For example, the Black Panthers grew to collaborate with many other leading liberal social justice movements. Protest celebrities such as Jane Fonda, Ralph Nader, Joan Baez, Angela Harris, Bob Dylan, Jesse Jackson, Teddy Kennedy, and Bob Marley were involved in headlining many of these protests either in person or in other more remote ways. Thus, the UofMN newspaper and twin cities in general have remained a center for protest movements, even today.

> ***Side note:*** *Years later, my daughter Anna became close friends with a St.Paul,MN high-school classmate and her family, whose mother (Sarah Jane Olson, née Kathleen Soliah) turned out to be a long sought fugitive from the anti-establishment social-justice protest group the Symbionese Liberation Army (SLA), the group that kidnapped heiress Patricia (Patty) Hearst and committed several criminal burglaries, bank robberies, shoot-outs, and bombings. During Anna's early college years, Sarah Jane was finally caught and arrested. She pleaded guilty as part of a plea-bargain to drop other charges, then later tried to plead innocence. She eventually did some prison time. But before that, Anna spent lots of time at their house during her high-school years, and even went with them on a remarkable vacation trip to New York's Manhattan district including museums, Broadway, and Central Park for a week. I guess we all have some stories that are bigger than most of us realize, or that we are willing or able to tell, without some outside help or encouragement.*

I was not born into or close to any wealth, status, or fame. My parents are mostly the second and third generation of Scotch-Irish, Scandinavian, and German-Austrian immigrants who came to America seeking subsistence-level agricultural opportunities. My father came to Minnesota's Mesabi Iron Range to work most of his life as a maintenance mechanic in the various minerals operations.

Both my parents were born and grew up in north-central Minnesota, my dad in Brainerd, and my mom about fifteen miles to the north and west. Both passed G.E.D. diploma testing at middle age, because neither had graduated high school in their youth. My mother's rural farm school house only went through seventh grade, and my dad quit after finishing sophomore year in high-school to enlist in the WWII U.S.-Navy after working in the big railroad repair shops in Brainerd until his seventeenth birthday.

Since nobody in my extended family had previously ever taken or aspired to four year college coursework, I was more "easy going" and not the most highly motivated high school student. But, I somehow showed enough aptitude in science and math to get a four year scholarship towards minerals engineering at the University of Minnesota. I also got three summer internship jobs; first at National Steel, and then two summers at U.S. Steel Quality Control and Ore shipment operations. These internships were crucial to paying for the rest of the costs of my university studies.

"When the gales of November come early"

—Gordon Lightfoot

Steel is a dominant material in most buildings, roads, railways, bridges, tunnels, water supply systems, sewers, ships, trains, cars, trucks, machinery, tools, appliances, and weaponry. Thus, it's always been an essential and dominant material throughout modern/postmodern times, nations, developments, and especially during wartimes. U.S.Steel Corporation (USS) dominated worldwide steel production for well over seventy years (1901-1980) and its parent-predecessor (Carnegie Steel Works) dominated for decades before that. Both USS and Carnegie grew to dominance by heavily tapping Minnesota Iron Ore production.

Both US and Europe still dominate in some specialty steels, stainless steel alloys, and some specialty fabrications, but today USS is just the 38th largest steel producer in the world, with many Aisian steel firms (China, India) passing it, as well as several large scrap-steel recycling firms. And, many more steelmakers are growing faster, thus they too will soon pass

USS in raw steel production. To say the least, my career along with many Minnesotans was drastically affected by these trends.

At USS Quality Control, all ore loaded to railcars was 'sampled' and all samples analyzed and assayed in the QC Chem Lab. My job was to assist in many QC-clerical duties, including sending teletype messages to both the DM&IR railroad and Ore Boat operations as to which railcars should go into which ore-boat, and whether that railcar needed to be "blended" (if higher in Phosphorus or Silica). I also recorded cumulative tonnages and running assay-averages for each completed ore boat.

During my two summers at USS, I calculated and recorded the ore load totals for many different ore boat-shipments. I recorded loads for the SS Edmund Fitzgerald dozens of times, because it was a prominent workhorse of the fleet. Nicknamed: Titanic of the Great Lakes or Pride of the American Side she carried 26,000 long tons of iron ore each run. Mighty Fitz also had two luxurious guest staterooms for passengers, usually iron and steel executives and their families. Several of my older colleagues at USS Quality Control told me about touring the Fitz including the guest quarters. They were even told they could put their names on the waiting list for a trip, of course it was unlikely they would be chosen.

November 10, 1975, the day she sank was only a little over a year after my last duties at USS. I had recently graduated and was working in underground coal for Consolidation Coal Company, called Consol. I remember hearing about the wreck, and that the investigations determined that the Fitz had broken in half during unusual gale force winds and waves. I remember especially because my colleagues had told about the Fitz being refitted from coal-burning to fuel-oil and lengthened by welding an added section into the middle of her cargo hold.

The wreck was a shocking tragedy that sparked Canadian singer Gordon Lightfoot to write and record his hit song the next year. Several ongoing investigations were precipitated and many new regulations to improve safety within the Great Lakes shipping industries resulted.

USS eventually invested heavily in crude-oil and gas production and rebranded as USX. Steel remains a dominant industrial material and the U.S. will always be a major consumer of steel. But the U.S. will never lead in worldwide steel production, ever again. Even though until just the last few decades, the U.S. dominated raw steel production worldwide for well over a hundred years and always looked like it would never slip, especially as far and as fast as it has in just a few years. The same is true of many other strategic and industrial metals and alloys, which the U.S. has been dominant in for the past couple centuries, but now in some cases is not even a bit-player anymore, and may probably never be again.

I wrote my 183-page engineering senior design thesis, based upon an actual copper-nickel deposit in northern Minnesota. Even then, 45 years ago, several different feasible copper-nickel ore-deposits were known to exist within the lower boundary layers of the massive Minnesota-Gabbro geological formations. Each deposit contains significant levels of associated gold, silver, and platinum-group metals. Since postmodern trends towards electric-vehicles require highly-refined raw-nickel production, Minnesota may yet find itself as a critical metals producer for worldwide EV-batteries (Electric Vehicles).

The U.S. has managed to turn around its slippage in primary energy materials production (oil, gas, coal) and is succeeding at growing important renewable energies (wind, solar). However, turning around these losses in primary metals production will not be as easy, and in fact is highly unlikely now, especially in steel. Whether these losses will ever threaten our national defense or industrial strength is yet to be determined. In any case, it needs to be included in the long term considerations of all U.S. leaders and citizens.

COAL FIELDS AND ENERGY CRISES.

As I was growing up, my father struggled with layoffs and economic downturns. Thus, he had to work as many hours as he was able to. He worked many extra shifts, over time, an overseas job with Thule Air Force base construction in Greenland, and he took risks and extra initiative to work in pulpwood trucking (buying a used truck, he fabricated a hydraulic pulp-wood loader, by welding and copying from a commercial loader), and various contracted out home remodeling projects on the side. He also did volunteer church work to help support me and my four sisters, and many other family, community, and church service projects together with my mother.

I really needed to fully support my own schooling costs through employment, scholarship, and some loans. Thus, I completed my engineering degree in 1975, precisely within four years as planned, received two job offers, and immediately took the higher paying offer at Continental Oil's Consolidation Coal Division in eastern Ohio, with prospects for new western coal projects in the Powder River Coal Basin. Consol had by far the greatest volume of coal under leases in the Powder River basin, but all of their leases were in Montana, where there was state opposition to coal expansion, whereas the first and biggest mines opening in that basin ended up in the Gillette Wyoming area.

To compound this, most of my early assignments were in three of Consol's eastern Ohio underground mines (near Cadiz, OH), where radical elements of the United Mine Workers union were in the midst of frequent and frivolous wildcat strikes. I had already worked in the steel industry where the USWA steelworkers union and local units were no pushovers as well as where my dad, uncles, and other close relatives and friends had spent their careers, including many large lay-offs, labor strikes and other issues. But, I never expected anything as belligerent and radical as I encountered in those underground coal mines.

Early in my work there, several union mine workers repeatedly threatened my life. They claimed they could easily hide my body under rock debris in the back exhaust tunnels and nobody would ever find me. Several of them actually lit and smoked cigarettes in front of me underground, which was then a serious federal offense in all U.S. underground coal mines.

They obviously did it to test me, and asked me outright, what are you going to do about it? It would have been a very big deal, if I would have reported it. So, instead I told them right then in front of several other workers, "No, I'm not going to report anything now, because we aren't near any new coal faces," (where there might be explosive methane gas present). "But," I said, "you should not even be carrying those matches and cigarettes down here. So, I and the other managers will be watching you two very carefully, and if I ever even suspect you or any of you others are carrying such smoking materials on you near a production coal face, whether you light up or not, I will have you searched, the materials taken, and I will personally report you to the company bosses here, at the union, and at the local federal MSHA offices." I never saw any cigarettes underground after that.

I tried to explain that my people, including my dad, were union iron-ore workers, USWA steel-workers union. A few did finally become friendly towards me. One was a former college football player who had tryouts with the nearby Pittsburgh Steelers NFL team.

I hated the way many people treated each other in those mines. One Friday morning after I had worked seven straight midnight shifts, I was really looking forward to starting my precious four day long weekend break. However, the assistant mine superintendent asked me to report on some wildcat strikers who were absent or had left during that midnight shift.

I stayed over long enough to pass the info to the mine clerk, and told him that I was leaving so he could finish the report with the info that I had produced and provided. He quickly ran to the superintendent who said if I left he would charge me with insubordination and have me fired. I said good, I am tired of working here anyway. The next week I was transferred to a different mine, but I wasn't fired. Division HR agreed with me that the mine management had HR problems much bigger than just me.

One cold winter Monday I came into work and the superintendent's car was sitting there wrecked from a rollover. The Friday night before, he had been at the local bar and pulled a knife on several union workers because of a drunken argument. Instead of backing down, they came after him so he ran to his company car and raced away with them close behind. After he crashed and rolled over in his car, they apparently decided to quit pursuing the argument.

Those were very turbulent times in the U.S. coal and energy industries. The OPEC oil cartel brought supply shortages and huge price hikes, so dramatic increases in coal production were forecast. But, new federal safety and health regulations made these production increases more difficult and costly. The labor unrest, wildcat strikes, and violence brought uncertainty that also hurt overall production. The recent former president of the UMWA, Tony Boyle, was being tried and convicted for murdering his rival, Jock Yablonski, a few years earlier in nearby Pennsylvania during those years, and not far away at this very same time the immensely powerful and notorious Teamster union leader, Jimmy Hoffa, disappeared never to be found.

I started looking for other jobs. I was offered a position at the local Ohio MSHA office within the US Dept of Labor, but instead, I moved back to Minnesota, and took the other job offer I had gotten even before graduating, at a federal minerals research center, but for a fifty percent cut in pay. My employer there was the U.S. Bureau of Mines, started in 1910 as one of the earliest federal bureaus, because mining and minerals were so important to the U.S. economy back then. By the end of the twentieth century, Tea-party Republicans looking to slash the federal budget had entirely eliminated the Twin Cities Research Center where I worked, along with the entire historic agency, the U.S. Bureau of Mines.

THE U.S. BUREAU OF MINES.

During the nineteen plus years at TCRC research, I wrote hundreds of research proposals for Advanced Mining Systems, each with important rationale and justification of the value to the nation needing to expand coal production and efficiencies, as an important stop-gap to the national energy crises during those years. Because of my recent and unique experiences in underground coal, I included many anecdotes about the human elements in so many of these inefficiencies. Within a few years of ranking my proposals, USBM started a new program called Human Factors Research. They did not put it under my control, of course, but because of my ideas and proposals, they encouraged me and involved me in the planning and hiring of managers and staff to conduct these new projects.

I took over seventy-five credits of graduate level coursework in various industrial engineering, psychology, management, and systems engineering to get more background in human behavior and ideas to manage such resources better. Most of the courses were taken without acceptance into any graduate degree program. I eventually applied and was accepted, however my credits were scattered in too many diverse disciplines, so I never did get a Master's degree in anything.

Lucky for me, the closure of the U.S. Bureau of Mines didn't occur until after I married Janet. It would bring over ten years of serious difficulties, because my degree in Minerals Engineering and my resume citing nineteen years work in federal minerals research subjects was not a clear match with any major work efforts going on in industry at that time.

I had designed, built, and promoted several database applications for resource planning of mining system maintenance operations, and I had worked with industry committees in support of various industry consensus standards for quality and safety. Thus, I took courses to get several relevant certifications being used within industry at that time.

These certifications took time and money, and during that time I assisted a younger USBM colleague who had patented a novel magnetic iron-ore separation device, and gotten federal approvals to commercialize it for sale to industry. I helped build and test two different sized prototype reactors, and also wrote a quality systems manual compliant to the ISO-9001 quality systems standard of that timeframe. I did not take any pay for this work, as there was no income yet generated by that project and company (5R Research). I had to draw and spend huge chunks from my retirement savings to get through that time, but I do not regret the struggles and efforts I made during those times. As I said, lucky for me I was then married to Janet. That was over twenty five years ago, and already I was pondering and taking notes for a possible book that I might write about our stories someday.

During the ten years of bootstrapping my career, back from this federal-career disruption, I had a child-support obligation calculated based upon my senior-salary of over 19-years seniority and promotions. I could have sought to reduce that obligation based upon so many short-term work assignments and job-losses. However, I never missed one payment, and never reduced the levels of those payments. Please confirm this record with both the state of Minnesota and with my ex-wife. In fact, I decided to keep paying tithing at that senior salary, so God would have to somehow restore me to that senior salary, or see me go bankrupt. I currently get zero federal pension from those 19-years service (and my social-security is low because federal workers back then paid zero social-security taxes in-lieu of their federal pension payments). I was able to survive those years by taking a total withdrawal option upon federal termination. It destroyed my retirement income prospects and has kept me working past 68-years old, but I have never really had to regret those decisions. (There's really never any complete retirement for faithful LDS anyways.) And, I truly believe the inspirations found within this book, and that helped me persevere to produce and finish it, have come from those faithful sacrifices way back then, which makes it more than worth it for me.

Eventually I did get work in short-term consulting and contracting in IT testing and validations, establishing and certifying ISO-9001 quality systems, FDA systems validations and process validations, and training and implementing various database applications for Enterprise Resource Planning, especially for equipment maintenance and repair work. These early bootstrapping efforts and jobs were very sporadic, risky and short-term, with almost no employment benefits package most of the time. They involved a lot of travel, and eventually required us to move to North Carolina for over five years, then to New York for three more years before moving back to Minnesota again.

I got to work with some fantastic R&D and production companies in pharmaceuticals, biotech, vaccines, monoclonal antibodies, implantable medical devices, deep-brain stimulation, heart-pacing systems, orthopedics, stents and catheter systems. I got to work within high-level multidisciplinary teams on incredible science and engineering challenges. We got to learn together as we actually built and tested components and assemblies for use. We got to learn from each other as we reviewed and approved each other's reports and documentation.

When I look back on my long fragmented career, including my many educational stumbles and my many job losses and disruptions; I consider it all a huge journey of miracles and blessings. I don't regret any of it, especially the hardest parts. They say we learn the most from testing ourselves even to find our mistakes and weaknesses, and I certainly got many chances for that. I would love it if you would consider my story as a witness and testimony that it is true: We absolutely do learn the most from our testing, our struggles, and even our stumbles and mistakes. These make up our diverse individual struggles, and our most important stories.

Early in my marriage to Janet, we were visiting family in northern Minnesota with all five of our children. On Sunday we had some spare time to worship with the little Grand Rapids branch of the Church of Jesus Christ of Latter-day Saints.

They were thrilled, and asked us to speak in each meeting. When they found out I was from the area, and I was a minerals engineer with vast experience in the iron and steel industries, they couldn't contain their hopes that we could move and strengthen their little branch. Now, over 25-years later, I hope these stories can indeed help their little branch, and hundreds of other little congregations like theirs.

PART 4

SUMMARY AND CONCLUSIONS

"STRUGGLES MAKE US STRONGER, SO THE BEST IS YET TO BE!"

Throughout this book, I have repeatedly promised, "the *best* is yet to be..."

In fact, I repeatedly qualified the unrestrained optimism of that statement with, "struggles make us stronger, so the *best* is yet to be." Since Janet's early childhood struggles were a bit harder than most, and those early struggles found many diverse ways of repeatedly cursing her, Janet is a good test example of whether those optimistic statements and promises can actually hold true, given today's modern challenges and uncertainties. I believe they can, and I believe that Janet's example provides great evidence and proof that they can.

FAMILY HISTORY FINDINGS.

During Janet's years at Ball State University in Indiana, she frequented Shively Hall which was part of a prominent building complex there, and matched the name of one of her prominent family lines. Senator Benjamin F. Shively was a prominent U.S. senator from Indiana at the turn of the century (1900) and was almost chosen as Wm Jennings Bryan's running mate in his presidential runs.

Janet did research through Familysearch.org, Ancestry.com, and other genealogy sites. She found that Senator Shively was not in her direct bloodline, but they are connected through a brother of one of her direct G.Grandfathers. She also found many links to "Church of the Brethren" and a direct bloodline to Alexander Mack, who was the top leader of the Schwarzenau Brethren who were spawned out of the radical-pietist revival during the Anabaptist movements in Europe, then came to Germantown, PA and helped start the beginnings which eventually became the Church of the Brethren.

And, Janet helped me research farther back in some of my family lineages. I found that my G.G.Grandmother Barbara Ann Gier and her parents had embraced the Book of Mormon in the 1850s living in western Iowa and eastern Nebraska. They joined the Reorganized Church of Jesus Christ of Latter-day Saints after the mainline LDS had left trekking to the Salt Lake valley. Some of the Gier's relatives and friends did join with the mainline LDS and thus trekked west earlier also.

At 18 yrs-old, Barbara Gier helped a neighbor family (the Leepers) with three little children as the mother was experiencing severe difficulties during her late pregnancy. The mother died during delivery, but the new baby lived. So, Barbara stayed on to help the father and his now four children, including the newborn. She eventually married him and raised those four children, and had two babies of her own. The first was Elsie Leeper, my Great Grandmother. The second, Claude, died in infancy. My father was named after Claude, and so my middle name comes from him also.

John Wakefield Leeper was a Civil War veteran and over fifteen years older than Barbara, so when he died she sold that farm and traveled to Minnesota in a covered wagon, with Elsie and her youngest step-children. When the children were fully grown and independent, Barbara went to the Dakotas to help her younger sister's family. Her sister had a "breakdown" from severe life-stress on the harsh North Dakota prairie and was institutionalized the rest of her life. Thus, Barbara helped raise her four children also. I look forward to meeting her beyond the grave. She must be a wonderfully strong and generous woman.

As I dug deeper into Barbara Gier's family, I found Quakers who farmed in Guilford County North Carolina but didn't like or participate in the slavery of those times. They possibly helped the Underground Railroad because many Quakers did. Regardless, they wisely left the South together with other Quaker families prior to the Civil War, first for Ohio, then Indiana, Illinois, Iowa, then Nebraska. Her lines included Herman Husband, a courageous pre Revolutionary-war patriot, whose direct posterity includes Husband Kimmel, the top admiral in charge of Pearl Harbor on the day of that fateful WWII attack on our US Navy Fleet headquarters.

CHAPTER 11

FINDING SPIRITUALITY WITHIN

(WHETHER WE BELIEVE IT IS GOD OR NOT)

Of course, if you have read this far, you know that Janet and I both believe that the "spiritual peace or voice within us" is God (the God of the Bible). So far, we have been vague about that, because obviously everyone needs to find and decide that for themselves, and although I will continue to leave that open, I will now detail a few of my specific beliefs in this Chapter 11, as a fulfillment of my promises and suggestions towards creating and maintaining a "Theory or Story of Everything".

OUTSTANDING INFLUENCES FROM THE BIBLE.

Some of the world's greatest poets and writers exhibit many significant influences from the Bible: Chaucer, Dante, Shakespeare, Donne, Hawthorne, Melville, Dostoyevsky, William Blake, T.S. Elliot, and William Faulkner to name a few, all bear huge biblical imprints within their works.

John Milton's works are permeated with scriptural themes, echoes, stories, and images. His epic English poem, "Paradise Lost" is not only profoundly influenced by the Bible, but has also influenced how many now and forever will view the Bible's heaven, hell, and Satan.

Shakespeare's writings are mostly secular in nature. He was predominantly a secular playwright who tried hard to capture the quirks and weaknesses of kings and buffoons, of tragic heroes, and of merciless villains. Yet, he used over 1300 documented Biblical references in his thirty-seven plays written from 1589 through 1613.

Obviously, he was well read and educated in the Bible. Obviously, his mind was filled with the language and images of the Bible. He seemed to expect that those who saw his plays would be able to get the level of meaning in his use of that Biblical language and those images that they brought to those dramas.

Being a brilliant and dedicated English major, these important literary influences have repeatedly attracted Janet to try to understand the Bible as much as is humanly possible. Thus, her lifelong studies and re-readings of the Bible, and her encouragement to me to do likewise.

Recap: Even before Chapter 1, (in the opening for Part 0) I encouraged everyone to find and tell of your own personal courage, your own personal story. I described how it would take patience and courage, to really dig deeper, through and beyond our "normal masks and acts" that we all develop and put on to be what others and the outside world around us want and expect us to be.

I described how Janet found God within herself, within the "still small inner voice" even before she knew or understood that it was actually God within her. I encouraged everyone to seek and find that voice or peace within, but cautioned that it never comes exactly the same, or without some associated struggles.

Each person needs to develop their own faith and confidence that they can hear or feel that inner voice or peace within themselves. And, even then, they should expect it to be somewhat different for them each time. This was true for Janet and me, as it will be true for you and everyone.

I described how Janet's inner voice helped her survive, but also helped her find that elusive yet genuine patience and courage that she needed to know and act in her destined, fore-ordained, roles and purposes (see "Janet's Dream" in the Appendix). Hers was to protect and care for others within her immediate scope (Lynn, her parents, and herself) because her parents had chosen to act so selfishly, they were in eternal danger, even from themselves.

ANCIENT RELIGION AND POLITICS; SEEKING A UNIFIED THEORY OR STORY OF EVERYTHING.

All of the four major formal religion-groupings of today (Christianity, Islam, Hinduism, and Buddhism) can trace some of their sacred records and traditions back to ancient times. In fact, Christianity, Islam, Judaism, and many other related minor faiths all trace back to a common ancestral lineage of Abraham and to his ancestors, stories, testimonials, and traditions, mostly found in the book of Genesis.

Similarly, Hinduism, Buddhism, Jainism, Sikhism, and many other related far Eastern faith groups all trace to various degrees from common sacred Dharmic records, stories, testimonials, and traditions. Although each of these major religion groupings have brought forth great positive contributions in the areas of literature such as inspired wisdom, poetry, and satire, as well as health, cultural arts, music, morality, law, politics, business, economics, and science. However, each of them has also historically contributed great negative contributions and evidences of corruption, abuse, hypocrisy, and violence by their adherents, and especially some of their more self-serving or alarmist leaders, throughout history.

Within each of these major religion groupings, there seems to have existed constant potential for both good and bad behaviors, good and bad interpretations of the religion, and good and bad leaders, who commonly used verbal influences and persuasions to attract and build support and power from their followers. For example, some teachers and leaders use their influence and persuasions primarily to create division and fear vs. unity and faith, rumors and half-truths vs. wisdom and kindness, quick-easy popular pathways and promises vs. longer, harder moral pathways, exclusionary practices vs. inclusive teachings, radical words vs. respectful actions, and anti-authority vs. pro-authority. Thus, they were often able to quickly build support and power from their followers. But in time, such short-term successes always eventually failed.

On the other hand, each of these major religion groupings has had many adherents who suffered and sacrificed greatly for their faith, often at the hands of those mentioned above, who were creating division and exclusiveness by using verbal zingers of fear and divisiveness.

THE EARLY APOSTLES:

I have described Janet's intensive interest and lifelong studies within the Bible. Of course, she was (and still is) interested in the many stories of "transforming" love, patience, and courage. And, the stories and words of the early Apostles (especially Peter, John, and Paul) are favorites of hers. Certainly, they in turn gained courage and patience from the divine words and examples of Jesus Christ (and Jehovah in the O.T.). Furthermore, they obviously had rare and eternal wisdom and perspectives of God and of Christ and how everything fits within God's plan for us within the Creation, the Fall, redemption through the atoning sacrifice of Christ, and the coming Judgements and Resurrections of all people who have ever lived on this earth.

Janet points out that much of this wisdom, knowledge, details, and perspective existed within the Old Testament scriptures, but was and is intentionally hidden or "veiled" by God within the stories, prophesies, examples, patterns, similes, allegories, parables, and symbolic metaphors. Jesus taught that "faith" is an important spiritual principle, and that such faith shouldn't be rushed, otherwise such faith can be frustrated and even lost if key spiritual wisdom and knowledge are counterfeited or short-cutted.

For example, the fullness of Christ's gospel has often been diluted, or "watered down" until it has lost much of its magnificence and power. Such a diluted gospel isn't so much non-Christian or anti-Christ, as it is a lesser counterfeit to the total fullness of Christ's gospel.

> The Bible says God has given all people this mortal life to become more like Him. Those who are true and faithful in all things will sit in the throne of Christ (Rev 3:21).
>
> They will have the name of God the Father placed upon them (Rev 14:1).
>
> They shall be "heirs of God, and joint-heirs of Christ" (Rom 8:17).
>
> What shall the faithful inherit? *All things,* according to scripture (Heb 1:2).

"Be ye therefore perfect, even as your Father which is in heaven is perfect." (Matthew 5:48)

"For I (am) the LORD that bringeth you up out of the land of Egypt, to be your God: ye shall therefore be holy, for I (am) holy." (Leviticus 11:45)

"Beloved, now are we the sons of God, and it doth not yet appear what we shall be; but we know that, when he shall appear, we shall be like him; for we shall see him as he is." (1 John 3:2)

"Verily, verily, I say unto you, He that believeth on me, the works that I do shall he do also; and greater (works) than these shall he do; because I go unto my Father." (John 14:12)

"God standeth in the congregation of the mighty; he judgeth among the gods... I have said, Ye are gods; and all of you are children of the most High." (Psalms 82:1,6)

For instance, no less prominent a modern Christian theologian than C.S. Lewis recognized the important logical and theological extension of being transformed by Christ. *"The Son of God became a man,"* Lewis reminded us, *"to enable men to become sons of God."* Further, Lewis has identified:

"The command Be Ye perfect is not idealistic gas. Nor is it a command to do the impossible. He is going to make us into creatures that can obey that command. He said (in the Bible) that we were 'gods' and He is going to make good his words."

—C.S. Lewis, *Mere Christianity.*

The Bible subsequently teaches:

- We were created in the *image of God*
- God is the *father of our spirits*
- We are the *offspring of God*
- Christ clearly calls us *gods*
- Man has become *as God*

- We will inherit *all things*
- We will be *co-heirs with Christ* of all things
- We will have *glory*
- We will have *thrones*
- We will be filled with the *fullness of God*
- We will be partakers of the *divine nature of God*
- We will be *one with God*
- We shall be *like Him*
- Our bodies will be fashioned *like His glorious body*
- We can even gain *perfection*
- *Jesus Christ* is the "Key", and the only "Way" to fully understand, or to receive any of the above.
- The *Old Testament* people were far more 'Christian' than even we Christians understand today, as those O.T. scriptures provide a second more ancient witness and testimony to fully understand the many diverse and vital divine roles and importance of Jesus Christ.
- Wesleyan (Methodist) theologians detect the influence on John Wesley from the Eastern Fathers, who saw the drama of salvation leading to the *deification (apotheosis)* of the human, in order that the *perfection* that was originally part of human nature in creation but distorted by the fall might bring fellowship with the divine. See: https://oimts.files.wordpress.com/2013/01/oxfordnotes1-5.pdf

"And God said, Let us make man in our image, after our likeness:" (Genesis 1:26).

"Furthermore we have had fathers of our flesh which corrected us, and we gave them reverence: shall we not much rather be in subjection unto the FATHER OF SPIRITS, and live?" (Hebrews 12:9, emphasis added).

"For in him we live, and move, and have our being; as certain also of your own poets have said, For WE ARE ALSO HIS OFFSPRING" (Acts 17:28, emphasis added).

"Forasmuch then as we are the offspring of God, we ought not to think that the Godhead is like unto gold, or silver, or stone, graven by art and man's device." (Acts 17:29)

"I have said, YE ARE GODS; and all of you are children of the most High" (Psalms 82:6, emphasis added).

"Jesus answered them, Is it not written in your law, I said, YE ARE GODS? If he called them gods, unto whom the word of God came, and THE SCRIPTURE CANNOT BE BROKEN;" (John 10:34-35, emphasis added).

"He that hath an ear, let him hear what the Spirit saith unto the churches; TO HIM THAT OVERCOMETH WILL I GIVE TO EAT OF THE TREE OF LIFE, which is in the midst of the paradise of God" (Revelation 2:7, emphasis added).

"Blessed are they that DO HIS COMMANDMENTS, that they may have right to the tree of life, and may enter in through the gates into the city" (Revelation 22:14, emphasis added).

"Neither pray I for these alone, but for them also which shall believe on me through their word; THAT THEY ALL MAY BE ONE; AS THOU, FATHER, ART IN ME, AND I IN THEE, THAT THEY ALSO MAY BE ONE IN U.S.: that the world may believe that thou hast sent me. And THE GLORY WHICH THOU GAVEST ME I HAVE GIVEN THEM; that they may be one, even as we are one: I in them, and thou in me, that THEY MAY BE MADE PERFECT in one; and that the world may know that thou hast sent me, and hast loved them, as thou hast loved me." (John 17:20-23, emphasis added)

"And to know the love of Christ, which passeth knowledge, THAT YE MIGHT BE FILLED WITH ALL THE FULLNESS OF GOD" (Ephesians 3:19, emphasis added).

"According as his divine power hath given unto us all things that pertain unto life and godliness, through the knowledge of him that

hath called us to glory and virtue: Whereby are given unto us exceeding great and precious promises: that by these YE MIGHT BE PARTAKERS OF THE DIVINE NATURE, having escaped the corruption that is in the world through lust" (2 Peter 1:3-4, emphasis added).

"He that overcometh shall INHERIT ALL THINGS; and I will be his God, and he shall be my son" (Rev. 21:7, emphasis added).

"For as many as are led by the Spirit of God, they are the sons of God. For ye have not received the spirit of bondage again to fear; but ye have received the Spirit of adoption, whereby we cry, Abba, Father. The Spirit itself beareth witness with our spirit, that WE ARE THE CHILDREN OF GOD: AND IF CHILDREN, THEN HEIRS; HEIRS OF GOD, AND JOINT-HEIRS WITH CHRIST; if so be that we suffer with him, THAT WE MAY BE ALSO GLORIFIED TOGETHER. For I reckon that the sufferings of this present time are not worthy to be compared with the glory which shall be revealed in us" (Romans 8:14-18, emphasis added).

"To him that overcometh will I grant to SIT WITH ME IN MY THRONE, even as I also overcame, and am set down with my Father in his throne" (Rev. 3:21, emphasis added).

"Who shall change our vile body, that IT MAY BE FASHIONED LIKE UNTO HIS GLORIOUS BODY, according to the working whereby he is able even to subdue all things unto himself" (Phil. 3:21, emphasis added).

"Beloved, now are we the sons of God, and it doth not yet appear what we shall be: but we know that, when he shall appear, WE SHALL BE LIKE HIM; for we shall see him as he is" (1 John 3:2, emphasis added).

"Be ye therefore perfect, EVEN AS YOUR FATHER which is in heaven is perfect" (Matt. 5:48, emphasis added).

> *"Likewise, ye husbands, dwell with them according to knowledge, giving honor unto the wife, as unto the weaker vessel, and as BEING HEIRS TOGETHER of the grace of life; that your prayers be not hindered"* (1 Peter 3:7, emphasis added).

ETERNAL SALVATION IS A LONG COMPLEX PROCESS, NOT A ONE-TIME EVENT OR DESTINATION.

The gospel of Jesus Christ is simple enough for little children to teach (understand) and be taught. Yet, in its fullness and details it is profound and complex enough to stump the most ingenious leading intellectuals.

From Janet's studies of the Bible, she often points out how lesser counterfeit gospel teachings seem to lead people to believe or understand a much lesser, easier, and shallower view of the gospel. Janet points to solid patterns and principles in the gospel showing repeatedly:

- The gospel is an entire *plan* and a long-term process, not a one time event or destination.
  - » (Without the Fall, there would have been no need for an Atonement or Grace. Thus, no need for a Savior or Redeemer, and the entire gospel plan would have been frustrated.)
- Repentance is an essential part throughout that entire process, not a one-time event.
- Eternal Salvation is a process, not a one-time event or destination.
- Perfection is a plan and a process, not a one-time event or destination.
- Creation is an ongoing process, not a one-time event.

THE CONCEPTS OF CIRCULAR (OR CYCLIC) CREATION AND REDEMPTION

Janet points to the Biblical pattern of "circular or cyclical processes." The seasons are cyclic or circular, life is circular, creation and everything in it is circular. Everything within eternity is circular (and eternity itself somehow has no beginning, and no end).

In my experience as a quality systems and quality assurance engineer every design-project is managed around a circular PLAN > DO > CHECK > ADJUST cycle that keeps revolving into a RE-PLAN > RE-DO > RE-CHECK > RE-ADJUST cycle until overall satisfaction is reached, and even then it is placed within an ongoing, yet simpler, more streamlined, but fully documented, fully audited and ongoing quality system for the entire lifecycle of the design.

Likewise, every design is first created spiritually (in someone's mind), then progressively through more physically tangible forms (sketches, drawings, blue-prints, scaled-models, mock-ups, prototypes, test-models, etc.) Each phase follows the circular PLAN > DO > CHECK > ADJUST cycle.

Thus, it makes total sense to me that a similar pattern was and is being used for eternal creations such as us, as well as a start or a beginning for a Theory or Story of Everything.

The Bible tells the story of a "War in Heaven" led by a rebellious archangel named Lucifer (aka. Satan, the Devil). This apparently happened some unknown eons of time before the Genesis stories of Creation, and the paradisiacal Garden of Eden, where Satan plays a role in bringing about the Fall from paradisiacal grace to a fallen state of separation from God.

In the War in Heaven story, Satan succeeds in drawing one third of the hosts of heaven to his side, leaving only two thirds staying with God's plan. So, what was Satan's plan? Undoubtedly, it was a lesser counterfeit plan that had features which were attractive enough that his many followers were willing to leave the almighty God's side for it.

Today as in ancient times, we see apostate religious leaders offering a quicker, easier, more politically popular gospel or religious alternative. Actually, we see greedy populist leaders on both the right and the left sides of the political spectrum seducing foolish followers into such flawed counterfeit thinking.

We have seen both socialist-communist and fascist leaders have great short-term success building large followings for their flawed promises. We have seen radical Islamist leaders doing likewise. Ancient Israel had repeated leaders who led the people away from the true-essence of their religion and towards a quicker, easier, more politically popular alternative.

Jehovah repeatedly called prophets and apostles to restore their religion, and they repeatedly rejected and stoned these messengers.

Today we see many megachurch televangelists who are selfishly seducing large followings towards their attractive prosperity-gospel alternatives. Likewise, many secular New Atheist leaders are selfishly seducing followers towards their attractive modern materialistic messages. Surely, any complete Theory or Story of Everything needs to include and explain these repeated (circular or cyclic) patterns.

ABOUT PUSHY "MOCKING" VS. "KILLING WITH KINDNESS"

Mocking certainly goes back to ancient times. In fact, it seems that every good idea gets mocked to some degree or another. And the better and very best ideas always seem to attract the most mocking in one way or another.

In the book of Genesis, Noah is mocked for around 400 years, as he patiently and courageously built his "Ark". Cain complains that he feels that God disrespected (or mocked) his religious sacrifice (and his career labors).

I suppose Lucifer must have mocked something about God's plan of Salvation as he was convincing one third the hosts of Heaven to his side, during the pre-Creation War in Heaven. Was it that his plan was quicker, easier, and more popular? Was it that God's plan involved much more time, patience, genuine courage, sacrifice and service to others, even undeserved suffering for the sake of others. Whereas Jesus' teachings and example to "love your enemies" and "do good to those that hurt you" are sure calls to try the "killing with kindness" alternatives.

Psychologists and sociologists have studied the most evil people and cultures compared to their most kind and benevolent counterparts. The premeditated intention to hurt others has likewise been a serious factor in determining criminal justice since ancient times.

Janet and I have tried hard not to conclude that anyone premeditated and intended to hurt us or anyone else. In fact, we both feel that even the thought of that kind of calloused intentional hurting would make it hurt even more, and make it less possible to patiently and courageously learn to just live with the pain.

WHAT WOULD JESUS DO?

Let's remember. Jesus always found ways to recognize and include the worth of everyone; especially the scapegoats and underdogs, the poor and sick, even the sinners, tax-collectors, publicans, and Samaritans. He attracted huge crowds, and included everyone in his teachings and blessings.

And beside his infrequent ministry to the big crowds, Jesus always demonstrated the importance of ministering to the "one". Even when He and His small group of disciples were traveling, or tired, or pressured by crowds, time-schedule, rough terrain, or other factors; He always seemed to demonstrate the importance of taking time to help or remember the forgotten or hated people. He would notice the poor, sick, needy, down-trodden, the trivialized or marginalized, and even the sinners, the hated tax collectors, and the publicans.

He didn't help them all at once in any kind of grand, showy miracle (except when he multiplied available food or wine to feed a large group). He taught and sent disciples out to minister two-by-two. And even though they lacked the faith to be as fully effective as He could be, each disciple could grow their faith by taking on such ministering assignments.

Jesus wisely avoided the over-zealous political disputes and opinions of His day, from the wicked and worldwide Roman Empires, to local King Herod issues, to the religious disputes between the Scribes, Chief-Priests, Pharisees, Sadducees, Essenes, or the violent local Jewish-zealots and revolts. He intentionally avoided them saying, "Render therefore unto Caesar the things that are Caesar's, and to God the things that are God's."

After healing and miraculously feeding the multitudes, many Jewish followers gathered and tried to forcefully make Him their earthly King. But their supposedly grand ideas for Him were selfishly flawed so He escaped their counterfeit ideas and worship to work out His own more meaningful and lasting pathway.

THE VIRTUE OF HUMBLE PATIENCE.

The year 2020 has become a difficult trial of patience for almost every person, in this entire big bad world of ours, and that's over 7 billion of us. An amazing feat for such a tiny virus such as the Covid-19 coronavirus.

Janet's story is also an amazing feat of humble patience. During Janet's surgeries, just before her divorce, a church leader who was impressed by her humble and patient faith, chose her to speak at a multi-stake devotional (a stake is like a diocese, so this event covered dozens of congregations, and possibly thousands of people). Janet was not yet baptized because she was still married to a man who was very opposed to her investigations. She prayed hard about what to speak on, when a thought occurred to, "just tell your story." So, when she felt a very strong spiritual witness saying "yes," she knew that is what she should do. She also felt a huge relief, because she had been very worried about this important event.

Janet has never feared public speaking like most people do. In fact, it comes to her so easily, almost as a gift or something. She taught school. She was the president of a prestigious women's club. It is a major reason this church leader chose her for this assignment.

When the evening of the devotional came, the church leader who had chosen her asked if she was ready. She calmly replied that she was, and that she had decided to merely tell her story. The church leader knew enough about her tragic abuse story that a look of worried shock or possibly horror came over him, and he said, "This is Christmas, and that's not what I asked you to do!" Janet calmly replied, "It's okay. I prayed about it."

As the event started and went on, she could sense a serious concern growing in the church leader before the keynote section, which included Janet's fifteen minute talk. Since Janet was not yet, at that time, a baptized member, she remembered and worried for him, possibly not knowing for sure if she could get the needed level of inspired revelation from the Spirit, especially to reverently tell the very worst aspects of her story.

I was not personally there that night. But, I know that she only related a very small portion of her personal story details that I have written here. I also know that she did an amazing job of telling it from her heart, from her own words and perspectives, and that she concluded and sealed it with the strong notion and testimony that she could not possibly have gotten through so much, without divine help from God.

I also know that talk had a profound effect on many people, because for years after our marriage, I would often hear people say, "Oh, you're the man who married Janet Jones!" or "He's the man who married Janet Jones!"

Janet's testimony that night included a strong focus on her faith in the Lord Jesus Christ, as the essential exemplar and the answer to all problems and questions needed to be included into any Theory, or Story, of Everything. Because Janet's story and divine testimony, then and now, began and continues through the Holy Bible, she always studies and mentions that first, before the Book of Mormon.

However, because of the serious divisions and problems of today concerning the Bible and the overall Christian movement, and because the Book of Mormon is truely "Another Testament of Jesus Christ" and literally mentions and authoritatively testifies of Christ in some way on almost every page (on most pages, multiple times), Janet and I both highly recommend and testify that the Book of Mormon is what it claims to be. And thus, please do not ignore it. Please find out for yourself about this "marvelous work and a wonder" (Isa. 29:14). We promise, you will never regret it, and you will never forget it.

PART 5

MORE ON OUR STORIES

WERE WE EVER, OR ARE WE NOW, MERELY SEEKING SYMPATHY?

I had originally included the following information into the earlier chapters of this book. But, it got to sounding a bit too negative, considering all things together. Nevertheless, I do need to include it here since it so closely relates to the stories shared so far.

CHAPTER 12

WE DID NOT INTENTIONALLY CHOOSE VICTIMHOOD, OR SYMPATHY SEEKING.

It's now been forty five long years since Janet met her first LDS missionaries. If you know how people with disabilities, who have worked hard and long to become as functional (or super-functional) as possible, may seem somewhat resentful of any kind of pity or sympathy, or being seen as victims. Well, that is a lot like Janet and I feel about our stories and the popular LDS opposition that we have faced.

We emphatically do *not* want any kind of pity or sympathy over any of it. In fact, we don't regret any of it, nor would we change any of it; not now anyway. We have worked very hard at healing and getting past these things; and sympathy from others has never been, nor will it ever be a big part of that healing. If some quick, simple, easy, popular sympathy was what we were seeking, we could have and would have simply fully resigned, and given in to the popular LDS opposition a long time ago.

Of course, our choice to continue our LDS investigations did contribute to many highly vulnerable underdog situations. Thus, we humbly and gently tried to adjust, but nothing seemed to help. We tried sacrificing and compromising. Somehow things just kept getting worse.

This story may seem exaggerated, whereas in actuality it has been pared down and many details simplified out that would have made it sound even worse. For example, Janet and I have both been actually confronted with several suggestions that we must have some strange martyr complex, always desiring to be the victims, supposedly to attract sympathy or pity, apparently like those mothers who maladaptively hurt their own children to get sympathy for themselves by proxy.

But then, per the LDS negativity, why did we both suffer and sacrifice so much for so long; and then lose our cherished marriages over it anyway? And why have we or our children never gotten any effective sympathy for these issues from anyone close to us? And why have we so often gotten unfairly and negatively treated, and blamed so much (consistently without fail by nearly everyone around us on both sides) whereas our ex-spouses and other close family have gotten all of the sympathy and popular moral support about those issues for the past forty years?

Maybe it is the other way around? Maybe they, and those people around them, who were (and still are) encouraging such unfair blaming and false assumptions for so many years should be psychoanalyzed for this strange idea of a pity party "martyr-complex"?

For example, we could quickly and easily create a list of dozens (probably hundreds) of people who could provide eye witness testimony of our ex-spouses and former close friends and family, both actively blaming and also repeatedly seeking and getting such unfair and unhealthy sympathy for and from each other (just start with Don and Vera, and both of our ex-spouses).

Conversely, I challenge you to find even one person within either of our families, who has provided any notable or significant sympathy to us or our children for these issues these past years. In fact, I challenge you to find anyone who has shown the courage to begin, or even attempt to begin the respect and understanding that it would take to effectively begin such.

And mega shame on anyone who has the audacity to suggest that Janet (or Lynn) intentionally sought any of the damaging abuse she received as a young child, or as a helpless fetus in her mother's womb. (Even a mother who selfishly smoked three packs a day for that entire nine month pregnancy, then complained and repeatedly blamed and shamed her own daughters when congenital malformations surfaced). But then as John always said about his piling onto the cruel bigotry of others, "What's the matter? Can't take a joke?"

I am sorry to sound so harshly judgmental. Most of our families have very little idea that Janet's childhood was so harsh and damaging. And, most of them cannot possibly understand the full dynamics and negativity around the anti-Mormon bigotry we have struggled under for so long. Even if they did somehow get it, they would surely risk the same falling on them, if they dared speak in our defense.

Another disturbing accusation kept getting repeated to us, yet we were never given any fair chance to fully answer or explain: that we (and all LDS members) are somehow so foolishly and snobbishly focused on personal "works" (like modern day Scribes and Pharisees, the ancient, snobbish church leaders, remember?) trying to "earn our way to Heaven", somehow ignoring the essential need for humble faith in Christ's divine Atonement, thus we are effectively and foolishly damning our own spiritual salvation.

I suppose they somehow see the long suffering of underdog persecutions, and faithful obedience to commandments adding to these damning "works". I personally believe that I, and all of my fellow Christ followers, need more humble faith and obedience, and less accusations and judgmentalisms.

Shame on those taking Jesus Christ's free and *inclusive* gift of divine Grace, and snobbishly pointing fingers at others who are so sincerely and innocently trying their very best to obey and honor their God and His divine plan for *all* (not just an exclusive, lucky few). But, each of you should form your own fair opinion on these judgmentally negative and snobbish accusations by the populist counter-cult ministries, media, and publishers.

After so many years of enduring such unfair and one-sided popular opposition, the repeated suggestions and harsh accusations that we were both acting as victims of our own struggles to get some kind of cheap, faked sympathy should be enough proof, by itself, to convince any fair minded person that something very wrong was happening here. (Perhaps diversionary cover ups? Maybe blaming us for our own struggles they helped cause, or added to, and then further victim shaming us about somehow, someway absurdly damning our own precious salvation?).

But, when others started subtly recruiting our own children and grandchildren into such damning and damaging conclusions, these extremely negative and hurtful suggestions absolutely had to be more fully answered from our side. Again, I am very sorry that it has taken me this long to more fully address these things from our side.

Seeking sympathy is absolutely not the intent of this book. Besides, any sympathy offered now would be at least decades after the time when it was most needed, and when it would have been most helpful. No, we gave up on such sympathy and respect long ago. And, as much as we could muster, we have since been humbly trying to have the best life that we can possibly have. In fact, we hope more than anything else now, that this book will be seen as proof of that kind of healing work and effort.

This book is also not about criticizing anybody else's faith. We have learned to love and respect the many diverse religious people we have met and befriended throughout the many travels, jobs, and locations that we have lived. We have also met and worked with many agnostics, the spiritual-but-not-religious, and those who have chosen no religious faith, or no faith in any God(s), most of which I've found to be confident, intellectually rational people, of relatively high moral and ethical standards.

> Note: I have worked with many PhDs, in research and in academia, and found a higher degree of skepticism over religion amongst them compared to people with more ordinary levels of education. I have agreed with their general skepticism of organized religion based upon the overall historical evidence. But, I believe the most popular new atheist-leaders and publishers are now deliberately ignoring and denying huge aspects of human-reality, based upon the legitimate lives, evidences, witnesses, and testimonies of billions of humans who have believed, and faithfully sacrificed enormously for their faith in God. In fact, most of the greatest human accomplishments ever, were produced by people who witnessed in one way or another that God helped them in such great endeavors. Conversely, no significant atheist leader or movement in the entire history of this world has ever produced anything other than massive human tragedy (e.g. USSR and other failed communist regimes) and that's not likely to change despite the enormous popularity of secular-socialist ideas.

After so many years of negative reactions to our LDS investigations, Janet and I both fully understand that many will always be skeptical and critical of our intentions. The Church of Jesus Christ of Latter-day Saints has always boldly pursued ambitious efforts to respectfully tell its message of the restored gospel in these latter-days. That clearly hasn't changed and I expect never will. We now understand how intensely threatened some will always be, because of those pursuits, and because of our connections to those pursuits.

However, that emphatically is not the subject or intention of this story, or this book. But again, if any of you insist upon making that accusation, please feel free to knock yourself out about it. It will be nothing new to us, as this story emphatically shows. In fact, I am pretty sure that I can now turn any such objections or oppositions into confirmations and endorsements for the importance of these stories, and of this book to a large market and network, which we will be regularly reaching out to.

I've never been given any kind of fair chance to tell -- let alone explain -- even a small portion of this story to my own family. Whenever I tried to gently explain even the smallest item or detail, I was always gang bullied, blamed, and shamed to a despicable degree of gang bigotry (of course, they always thought and claimed they were doing me and everyone a favor). That has to stop now, or the promotion of this book needs to dig even deeper and harder into these things, for everybody's sake.

As I said above, the reason Janet's story is so important and compelling to the entire subject of this book is because of the unusually vivid and illustrative examples of stark injustice and related shaming it presents for everyone. Most of those close to us have had no idea that her underdog story could possibly go back that far, and with that kind of terrible injustice and injuries. But, because the popular and subtle opposition always seemed to hold such status, power, and unethical authority in and around our situations, those people allowed it to warp their own personal opinions and judgment in anything related to us, including ever really listening or honestly seeking to know us and the depth of our struggles, feelings, and the damages caused by these matters.

But, I never wanted this book to be just about that particular popular opposition, or just about us. Thus, I started and ended this book with the general focus of repairing the American Dream, and on better understanding the effects of positive and negative rhetoric on everyone's faith, hopes, and ideals about the American Dream. Again, I mostly hope that our stories will provide examples and evidence that can help all of us understand and repair these things better, together.

WHY ME? WHO AM I TO CHALLENGE THE POPULAR ANTI-CULT MINISTRIES?

I am old, semi-retired, worn down, and I am absolutely not looking to lead any new church, organizations, or movements. Mostly, I am writing a book of stories, for my family, my children, my grandchildren to help anyone and everyone who might care to understand our stories, lives, and relationships better. I also hope these stories have value for the bigger, more universal issues and problems of our day; And I will surely try to participate and help anyone who becomes inspired by these ideas.

But, who am I to challenge the popular anti-cult ministries, calling the results of their ministries un-Christlike and unethical? They are apparently backed by churches, leaders, and alliances of supposed tremendous status, power, and authority, while even my own family have withdrawn and mocked my personal and religious insignificance. But, I personally cannot stay silent any longer, especially as husband to Janet, whose overall story of such levels of unjust treatment simply cannot be ignored anymore.

Those supposedly "united" ministries, churches, leaders, and alliances are not united more than mostly a kind of two faced, faked, and forced "unity". In 2017, there were 45,000 separately managed and recognized Christian organizations (groups, branches, denominations) worldwide (per The Center for the Study of Global Christianity) with an average of two and a half new ones divisively forming every day. Even the largest, most powerful and stable, established denominations are pathetically breaking into divisive pieces because of the hypocrisies and "interpretive pluralisms" their various leaders and patrons are continuously finding within their understandings (and misunderstandings) of their own Biblical translations and creeds. And, the rates of suicide, divorce, and depresion among pastors is disturbingly and increasingly getting higher with each passing year. But, is it those pastors' fault? Of course not; we all need to look deep inside of ourselves, to find and root out these divisive hypocrisies.

Given the prevalence of predatory "bad actors," especially among these new Christian and religious sects (and breakoffs) constantly being added to various "danger watch" lists kept by major governments around the world for concerns and evidence of unethical practices and coverups of serious financial extortions (as well as occasional and unfortunate child abuse, and sexual abuse) the current level of disharmony within global Christianity and as defended by the anti-cult ministries is shameful and unethical at best.

Their accusations and label of a "non-Christian cult" used towards the mainline Church of Jesus Christ of Latter-day Saints are not even officially acknowledged, mentioned, or confronted by that church's top leaders, as they seek to avoid contention, and humbly and patiently follow our Savior's inclusive teachings and example. So this opinion is clearly mine alone, and definitely not encouraged or approved by any LDS leaders (see the Disclaimer section at the beginning of this book). But, I have very carefully pondered all of these things for the past forty years of my related struggles, and I simply must tell these stories. I just cannot pretend they did not happen anymore, despite everybody (including LDS leaders) preferring that I not mention it so forcefully.

And I must personally object to this label: You simply cannot possibly create or find a more inaccurate, divisive, damaging, or derogatory label within U.S. society and religious culture than a "non-Christian cult," especially as it has impacted the lives and children of such vulnerable investigators as Janet and me. You might as well label us suckers and losers, victims and fools, and since we essentially have been so labeled, I cannot sit still any longer. Especially since the church and people of the mainline Church of Jesus Christ of Latter-day Saints are the last to ever deserve such a derogatory slur.

Since nobody else is going to, I am forced to try to explain what these divisive labels and elements have done to me and my family (and, I suppose, to many other vulnerable investigators over the years). The combined "odd couple" effect of Janet's and my stories, together with Janet's singularly remarkable childhood abuse stories give this book a kind of clout that few others have had in these regards.

Nevertheless, I strongly believe that despite these divisive issues diluting the ethics, morals, and authority of the entire Christian movement, that the authoritative use and interpretations of the Bible can still be united and rescued from this chaos. I will try to explain more, and provide some respectful ideas and solutions for this in future writings.

> NOTE: I will never suggest or propose any kind of elusive "utopia", or forcing (or more likely enticing) everyone to think alike, or the same (both have been tried in the past and proven to fail multiple times over). I believe that unity does not necessarily require robotic uniformity or even universal agreement. I will never ask or encourage you to give up your best hopes, faith, or principles for any kind of faked, or two faced unity or positivity.

CHRONIC PROBLEMS IN CONTEMPORARY CHRISTIAN WORSHIP MUSIC.

I am no expert on the loud new contemporary worship music, but at least some of it seems inappropriately irreverent and problematic to me. *"The Lord is in His holy temple: let all the earth keep silence (and reverence) before Him"* (Habakuk 2:20).

As I said earlier, the Bible has dozens of other similar verses clearly calling for deep reverence and quiet respect in the Lord's house, and while worshiping in His Holy presence. Yes, we sing sacred praises to Him (sacred hymns), but for the last several hundreds of years the sacred hymns and the instruments used to accompany them have always been designed to evoke quiet-sacred and reverent feelings of holiness and solemnity. Only in these last fifty years or so (especially recently), has Christian worship started deviating from that. Again, I am certainly no expert, but those who have studied to become the most-informed experts on these trends are finding serious problems. See the following recent video reports on these trends:

- https://www.youtube.com/watch?v=b6nSe8tPYw0,
- https://www.youtube.com/watch?v=afEF0xutg0Y&t=2218s
- https://www.youtube.com/watch?v=HhR0xm4pyso
- https://www.youtube.com/watch?v=uIwD7DiP1ig
- https://www.youtube.com/watch?v=H9Gn4zK7VUs

Again, I mention these problems and concerns, because the unwise and unfair judgments and hypocrisy they illustrate are so close to what Janet and I have quietly suffered and observed for so long about the anti-cult, or counter-cult ministries which kept coming against us and our children personally in one way or the other. Always using quick, easy, but very shallow and diluted-down rationale and tactics to discount and negate any of our feelings or perspectives.

REASONS WHY I AM ACTUALLY GRATEFUL FOR THE POPULAR OPPOSITION, AFTER ALL IS SAID AND DONE.

This content was listed years ago on www.lightplanet.com.

1. *"Thou shalt love thy neighbour as thyself"(Matt 22:39),* and *"But I say unto you, Love your enemies, bless them that curse you, do good to them that hate you, and pray for them which despitefully use you, and persecute you."* (Matt 5:44)
2. Their efforts generate interest in the Church, and keep it in the public eye, which helps our missionary work prosper.
3. They provide a unique insight into the life of the Savior and early Apostles by demonstrating what it must have been like for them to deal with Scribes and Pharisees.
4. They motivate us to study the peripheral, obscure, and markedly unimportant aspects of our religion.
5. They make us laugh with their obtuse, inane, dubious, nefarious, absurd, rancorous, and spiteful antics.
6. We get to dust off our Logic 101 books, and find application for the many fallacies we learned about in school.
7. They give religious bigotry a bad name.

8. Their "cottage" industry is a boost to local economies--particularly paper and print businesses; and their tracts provide a cheap source of fuel for wood stoves and fireplaces.
9. We are no longer left to wonder: "how many times can the same weak and well-refuted claims be made against our faith?" Infinity! "To what extent will the anti-Mormons go in forwarding their un-Christlike agendas?" Anything goes -- including "lying for the Lord".
10. They provide a loving "home" for the chronic discontents, and they help make even the most misinformed and unscholarly writers of religion feel important and erudite.

THE MAN IN THE ARENA

From the famously significant speech, "Citizenship in the World," given at the Sorbonne in Paris, France, by Theodore (Teddy) Roosevelt, April 23, 1910.

> *"It is not the critic who counts; not the man who points out how the strong man stumbles, or where the doer of deeds could have done them better. The credit belongs to* ***the man who is actually in the arena****, whose face is marred by dust and sweat and blood; who strives valiantly; who errs, who comes short again and again, because there is no effort without error and shortcoming; but who does actually strive to do the deeds; who knows great enthusiasms, the great devotions; who spends himself in a worthy cause; who at the best knows in the end the triumph of high achievement, and who at the worst, if he fails, at least fails while daring greatly, so that his place shall never be with those cold and timid souls who neither know victory nor defeat."*

STRUGGLES HAPPEN TO EVERYONE; SO TRY TO HAVE THE BEST, HAPPY LIFE YOU CAN.

Janet and I, understandably, have very serious doubts that anybody from our families, or from our childhoods will have any serious attraction or approval of this story, or book (forget any chance or wish on our parts for any kind of respect or sympathy from them; as those went down the drain a long time ago). In fact, a few of them are still very likely to get riled by them, and start blaming us again, as before. I am sorry about that, but am willing to take that risk, because these stories are far too important to not be told now.

But, we are quite sure that millions of the members of the Church of Jesus Christ of Latter-day Saints will have more than a passing interest in the dynamics of these stories. We are also quite sure that the many millions of those of other faiths and beliefs, that have come to highly respect, and more so to curiously befriend this Church and its members, will also have more than a passing interest. Thus, we promise to focus our book promotion efforts to those two very large groups.

In the end, these stories drove me most significantly to keep working to write this book. These stories needed to be told in a more complete way. Thus I realized they needed to be written, not just told orally.

Please forgive me for inserting so many of my personal ideas and opinions into these stories. Please understand that I have many more ideas and opinions that I did not include because I tried hard to refrain from doing so. Please understand that I want you to have your own confident views, and I encourage you not to be overly influenced by my personal opinions.

So, as my quirky narration of these important stories ends, I search for a proper closing. Since God and everyone else knows I'm not a poet, I'll borrow a few lines, by a fellow northern Minnesotan from the town I was born in:

"I'd go hungry, I'd go black and blue / I'd go crawlin' down the avenue / No, there's nothin' that I wouldn't do / To make you feel my love."

"When the evening shadows and the stars appear / And there is no one there to dry your tears / I could hold you for a million years / To make you feel my love."

—Bob Dylan.

APPENDIX

IN JANET'S OWN WORDS:

LOVING WORDS AND ACTIONS FROM GENERATIONS OF GRANDMOTHERS.

My dearest Katesy,

Fifty one years ago, in February 1970, the year I graduated from high school, my most beloved grandmother, Albertha Carolina Fritz (nee: Steffen), passed away on a Thursday afternoon of a bright early spring day in northern Indiana. Her neighbor, Pearl Meyers, wasn't feeling well that day and Grandma had taken lunch to her before noon. After she and Grandpa had finished their lunch, Grandma took a fresh piece of cake over to Pearl. On her way across the yard to return home, she looked up and waved and smiled at Grandpa, who was watching her from the window. Then, she collapsed on the snow spotted grass and died of a massive stroke before Grandpa could get to her side. She was sixty three years old.

We lived in Indianapolis then and it was a two hour drive from my grandparents home. We saw them several times a month and the weekend before that awful day, my grandparents had spent Friday, Saturday and Sunday at our house. They intended to leave on Monday morning, but when Lynn and I returned from school that afternoon, Grandma and Grandpa were still there!! A little snow was falling when they got ready to go, so they stayed. Lynn and I were so happy to get to have them for another day! Later, my sister and I decided that that extra day was a pure gift from Heavenly Father to us. My mother was often irritated or even angry at her mother, but for us, Grandma was the warm sun in our dark sky. She was a deep well of unconditional love and we were two parched children raised in a barren wasteland of abuse. We loved her fiercely. I simply cannot find the words to express the depth of my sorrow and loss at her death.

In 1984, our little family (John, me, Jennifer and Katie) were spending Christmas with my parents in northern Indiana. After all the presents were opened and Jennifer and Katie were playing with their new toys, my mother produced one last gift... for me. It was a small flat box and the tag said, "from Grandma". Inside, I found two pillowcases with embroidered flowers on them and beautifully crocheted edges. Mom explained that my dear Grandmother had been working on them as a graduation gift for me but that she had been unable to finish them before her shockingly sudden passing. Mom said that she had found a woman to finish the embroidery so now I could have the gift my grandmother had planned fourteen years earlier.

I have cherished these pillowcases. They have never been used. They have had a near-sacred place of honor in my heart. I hope you can understand how having this last gift, made by my beloved Grandma's hands, with her love in every stitch, has been like having her near me once again.

And now, my own precious and cherished, eldest granddaughter is graduating from high school, so it seems to be an appropriate time to hand down a symbol of love everlasting. I want you to have these pillowcases as a tangible bit of the legacy that is yours, of generations of women who are proud of you and the woman you are becoming. I cannot think of a better way to honor my Grandma or a better way to honor your present achievement. Never forget that you are sealed to be part of an endless line of "Grandmas" who are now placing their hands on your shoulders and, bending low, they all whisper as one, "Sweet dreams, dear Katesy, and may angels sing you to your future."

I love you so much, my darling granddaughter.

Love, from your Grammy.

JANET'S SPECIAL DREAM.

For a few years, when I was around thirty years old, I was a dreamer. I had a series of prophetic dreams during that time and then, they stopped, and I haven't had another one like them since.

In several of the dreams my husband appears as God-fearing, loving, and faithful to me, so I kept believing that John would change and become that faithful husband. Now as I look back on those times, I realize it was not John in those dreams. It was Bruce Nelson, of course.

They always began the same way. Someone came to my bedside and told me to come with them. I thought it was a man, although he never spoke and I never saw him. He would take us to a high place, and while he stood behind me, he would direct me to "look" and somewhere below us a scene would play out. It was almost like watching a movie, except I was in the movie, and I could observe myself moving and acting in whatever scenario was playing out below us.

In this particular dream, I am above a very large and grand hall. It is a beautiful and ornate space, filled with light, and there are people walking around inside it. The most notable thing in the hall was a very long line of doors along one side. Near the end of the line of doors, stood a most magnificent man who radiated wisdom and kindness. He was tall and imposing with long, dark wavy hair and there was a young woman standing next to him. My focus is directed toward those two people and I see that the young woman is me.

I watch as the man standing next to me makes a large sweeping motion with his arm. One of the doors directly in front of us swings open and the room beyond is revealed. It is dazzling and filled to the top with all the treasure of the earth. A bright golden light shines out from the room onto the floor where we stand and we can feel its warmth. Chests bursting with gold and silver and jewels, casks full to the brim with sweet wine and sheets of silks and fine-twined linens are piled to the ceiling. I sense that this room holds every good thing this world can offer...success, wealth, education, family, love. Everything I could ever want, or dream of, is within the walls of this room.

The man makes the same large sweeping motion with his arm again and another door swings open to reveal a second room. It is a dark and barren cell. The only light comes from a single, narrow, barred window high up on a hewn stone wall. It is cold and damp and forbidding. Instead of the abundance of the previous room, this room is like a vacuum, sucking any warmth and light in and giving nothing back. As I look into the dim, cheerless space, I know that it is filled with hardship, pain and sorrow. Misery and want, of the acutest kind, awaits anyone with the misfortune of being found in this desolate room.

After I have been shown the two rooms, the man beside me says, "You may choose either room." At that moment, I realize that he is showing me the circumstances of my birth and he is allowing me to choose between two stark realities into which I may be born. Then he speaks again and the words this time are very profound. He says, "You have earned the right to make this choice and you are worthy of either room." I think to myself, "How can I be worthy of both of these rooms? One seems to be a rich reward and the other a terrible punishment." I sense that being worthy, in this case, means that he believes that I am strong enough to succeed in either of these conditions. For me, this is a brand new way of seeing these situations.The man is presenting these two scenarios as merely ways for me to gain experience, bitter or sweet.

Strangely, I am strongly drawn to the barren cell. I know that this will be the place I will choose but I am filled with a sudden dread. What if it is too hard? What if I can't do it? What if I fail and I am not allowed to come back to stand beside this man again? Just as these questions are becoming nearly overwhelming, I notice that a group of people has gathered around us. They are intensely interested in the interaction between the man and me, and they are watching closely to see which choice I will make. My fear must have been obvious to them because someone steps out from the group and comes to stand next to me. She is beautiful. She wears her goodness and innocence like a glowing garment around her and although she is not particularly strong, she is very brave. She turns to face the man and she says, "I will go with her." The man nods and the deal is struck.

The beautiful, brave woman who stepped out from the group is my sister. I owe her everything. I owe her my very life. I chose the barren cell that we would be born into but she chose me.

HOW-TO NOT TREAT A FOUR YEAR OLD.

When I was just shy of my fourth birthday my family moved from Warsaw, Indiana to Indianapolis. My father had taken a job with the State Police and he had purchased a small house for us. My mother, five week old sister and I traveled in the family car with some household belongings, in what was probably the longest trip my mother had ever undertaken by herself. My newborn sister was on a blanket in the front seat and I was lying in the backseat with my mother's prized, long gray electrolux vacuum cleaner. When we arrived at our house, one of our new neighbors crossed the front yard to meet us and welcome us to the neighborhood. She saw immediately that I was alarmingly sick. A check of my temperature said it was 107 degrees. She called her pediatrician, and even though it was a Saturday, he drove right to our house. He put me in the backseat of his car and drove me straight to St. Vincent's hospital where I was seen by a urologist. Before he took me away in his car, he quickly told my parents to make whatever phone calls were necessary to get the family to Indianapolis, because he did not expect me to live more than a few hours if the doctors at the hospital couldn't help me. The specialist knew of a new drug, Furodantin, and he began treating me with it. He, and the new neighbor, saved my life. Someone reading this might wonder how it was that my two parents were not the people saving my life that day. I really don't have an answer except to say it is the first example, that I remember, of unusual parental disregard of my needs.

A few weeks after our move, and still before my fourth birthday, I was outside in the front yard, walking along the street. I was alone. The road in front of our house was barely wide enough for two cars to pass each other (which didn't matter because they rarely did) and serviced about ten houses. I had received strict warning about going onto the street and I was carefully avoiding the pavement. I was walking in a kind of "no man's land" in gravel and grass, beside the actual road. To my child's eye, I was breaking no rule and I remember delighting in the sound the gravel made when I stepped on it. I was imagining myself as a gunslinger, staring down my opponent in a deadly duel. Every step I took sounded just like boots on a dusty western street. My father came to the front door and called to me to come inside. When I came into the living room, I looked around for him but he wasn't there. Suddenly, he jumped out from behind the front door, where he had been hiding, and began to beat me with his belt for walking on the street. It was altogether terrifying and I have never forgotten it.

As an adult, I look back on these two incidents with a mix of emotions. My parent's detachment when I was so very ill could possibly be excused by a new job, a new baby, a move and a new house all happening at once. The second story, occurring only two or three weeks after my life-threatening kidney infection (which I was still being treated for) and intensive care hospitalization, is harder to explain away. Taken together, they present the beginning of a very troubling lack of normal parental care.

THE ULTIMATE BETRAYAL.

When I was growing up, both of my parents worked full-time, although it was unusual in the late 1950s for a woman to work outside the home. My sister, Lynn (four years my junior), and I were cared for, during the day, by a succession of women who needed some extra cash. For ten dollars a week, we were dropped off at a daycare home at 6:30 am and picked up again between 5:30 and 6:00 each evening. When I was eight years old the woman was Mrs. D. She and her family lived in a tidy brick home with a detached garage. In between the house and garage, the "D-family" had put in a breezeway with jalousie windows at both ends. It was uninsulated and unheated.

My four year old sister was left alone each day with this babysitter, while I attended school. Lynn suffered from extreme asthma and there was very little available at the time to treat it. Her little rib cage was enlarged from the effort to breathe and it gave her a hunched forward posture and she was smaller than other children her age. She could never run and play and she could not tolerate dust or cold temperatures. I don't recall her ever taking a silent breath; she always wheezed. Mrs. D was particular about her house and so she kept Lynn in the breezeway to prevent any disruption to her routine. She did make one allowance for the winter weather (this was central Indiana, where winter temperatures are often below freezing); she kept the door from her kitchen slightly ajar to let some bit of heat into that space. My sweet baby sister sat there, alone, with very few toys, until I came back from school. Each day, I would find her in her coat and mittens, chilled to the bone and struggling for breath. My heart breaks still, to remember how happy she was to see me. Each evening, Mrs D would bring us into the house, with strict instruction to sit quietly on the sofa, a few minutes before our parents were due to arrive. In this manner, she was able to conceal her neglect and callousness. I tried to tell my parents about how we were treated in that house, but I was not believed. After about a year with this family we moved on to the next place, the "L-household".

Virginia L had lots of children of her own (a plus in my book) and she was always drunk (another plus in my book...less supervision). I overlooked the fact that she had the added benefit of a fifteen year old son, Bruce, but I would soon become aware of my error in not considering him in my appraisal. They had a large one acre backyard and during our first summer there, Bruce put up a tent on the edge of the yard. Bruce was what little kids called, "a big boy". One day, he sent the other children off to hide, and he caught me by the wrist and declared that I was on his team and he pulled me into the tent with him to "count". I said that I did not want to be on his team; I wanted to hide with the others. It was no use. He had me and I couldn't get away. I suspected that he was going to tease and torture me the way I had seen other "big boys" do to little kids. That was not what was on his mind. I had to submit to his strange and disgusting desires. He threatened to really hurt me if I 'told' on him. After I was released, I made up my mind that I would never be in that tent again. I was so watchful and so careful but, of course, he caught me again. He stopped my desperate attempts to escape with a single quietly hissed statement; it was me or my sister...it made no difference to him. I was not ever going to allow him to do to my sister what he had done to me. So, at nine years old, I put my small body between that monster and my precious little sister. Day after day I was taken into that hot tent to endure his abuse. Finally, school started again and the tent came down. I thought I was free but no, I wasn't free. Although it didn't happen every day, Bruce still caught me in the hallways and pulled me into the bathroom with him when he could. He threatened that he and his friends would come to my house and get me if I ever told anyone. We only lived three blocks away so I believed him. I was scared all the time. Sometime during that winter, I decided to risk telling my mom. Late one night, I saw my chance. Dad went to their bedroom and Mom was still in the kitchen, alone. I crept out of bed and went out to her and blurted out that Bruce had been hurting me. She believed me but she wanted to know all about it. She was very thorough in her questioning. There was nothing that was too embarrassing or invasive to ask about. She spared me nothing. To this day, I feel more violated by my mother than by my abuser. But, at least I had been able to tell someone. Now, things would be better.

The next morning we were delivered to the same babysitter. And the next week. And the next month. Nothing. Ever. Changed.

And then, it was summer again and the tent was back up in the yard. On the first day of summer break, Virginia left us alone, with Bruce in charge while she went to the grocery. He was sixteen now and even bigger than the summer before. He caught me and carried me upstairs. He told the other children to stay outside. He turned on the vacuum cleaner so it sounded like he was doing his work. He took me into his bedroom. He knew more since he was older. It was worse than anything he had done before. I knew in my child's heart that I could not submit to him again. I just wasn't strong enough. When Virginia returned, I went straight into the kitchen where Bruce was helping to unload groceries and Virginia was putting them away. Right in front of that awful boy, I told Virginia what he had done to me. She went into a terrible rage...at ME! She screamed that I was a "lying little bitch." She grabbed a chair from the dining room and slammed it down in the middle of the kitchen floor and threw me into it, hard. She said I had better stay in that chair or she would "kill me, for sure." Her verbal assault continued through the day, even though she was drinking a lot. I remained in the chair all day, no food. No water. No bathroom breaks. Eventually, Mom and Dad came (at their usual time) to take Lynn and me home. We went out to the car and waited while they went inside. They had never done that before and I had a feeling that somehow they knew what had happened that day. After a few minutes they came out and got in the car. Mom turned around in the front seat and said with awful venom, "Je-sus CHRIST, Janet! Don't you know, good babysitters are hard to find?!" Then Dad followed up with, using the same terrible venom, "Why couldn't you just keep your goddamn mouth shut?!" I was ten years old.

And the next morning we went back to that same house. Well, you know, you have to finish out the week.

I wish this was my only story of parental neglect, dereliction of normal parental duty and callous disregard of the needs of their daughters. It isn't. It isn't even the worst story of the barbaric way we were raised. Through experiences like this, I formed some grim, foundational, assumed truths for my reality and world view.

I learned that: 1) I can not depend on anyone. 2) No one will defend me. 3) No one loves me. 4) I have no value. And 5) I am alone…

THE EPILOGUE

HOW WE BEGAN THE THINKING AND PONDERING ABOUT WRITING ALL OF THE STORIES AND IDEAS FOUND IN THIS BOOK.

ENCOURAGING EXAMPLES FROM AN EXCELLENT CURRENT WRITER.

Not long after losing the long-term - federal minerals research job in Minnesota, we found ourselves living and working in Greensboro, NC for over five years. There we struggled through several jobs, and many diverse short-term consulting assignments, before packing again for living and working in New York.

During our time in North Carolina, we were able to observe and know (they didn't know us) the prolific writer, Orson Scott Card, and his family. They attended church in a small congregation that used the same building as the Guilford ward, which we attended.

The Card family loved music and great literature, which was especially attractive to Janet. "Uncle Orson" loved to write ideas, and to inspire and encourage others to write, which was especially attractive to me. Orson boldly reviewed many different political policies and ideas in the local Greensboro newspaper, *Rhinoceros Times*, which also attracted me to seek and tell the story of everything, at least as I saw ideas that could explain and treat everything.

Janet's sister Lynn lived only a couple of hours away, in Chesapeake, Virginia. So, she and her husband and son would drive to our house for all holidays and many other weekends. It was a luxury of lots of time together, that Janet and Lynn hadn't had since their childhood. I encouraged them to talk freely about their parents. And, as I listened, I increasingly knew it was a story that had to be told, someday, somehow.

It was early one Saturday morning, soon after moving to Greensboro, NC when Janet woke me saying, "Listen, do you know what that is? It's a mockingbird going through his repertoire of sounds." Sure enough we soon discovered a nest built deep into a thick bush with long sharp thorns everywhere. Those mockingbirds continued to use that bush each year that we lived there. As I described before, our next door neighbors had a fat old cat that would lay in the shade beside their car sitting in the driveway. Several times we observed our two crafty mockingbirds go under the neighbor's car to torment that old cat by picking at his tail or other areas of his fur. It was such entertainment keeping up with those two very feisty, spunky mockingbirds.

Harper Lee's book, "To Kill a Mockingbird" would surely have been a good book even without its clever metaphor-title and reference to mockingbirds. But I'm not sure it would have become as great. The bestselling sheet-music, "Listen to the Mocking Bird" could surely have been successful even if it had been about a different species of songbird. But I'm not sure it would have become nearly as beloved. Likewise, I hope the "mockingbirds" will help this book become more interesting and helpful.

BEST SUPPORTING ACTOR - OSCAR AWARD.

During their childhood visits at Grandpa's farm, one winter weekend *Saturday Night at the Movies* was playing the 1949-film "Twelve O'Clock High" about aircrews who flew dangerous daylight bombing missions against Nazi Germany during the early days of American involvement in WWII. In this movie, Dean Jagger won the Academy Awards "Oscar" for Best Supporting Actor in playing an Air Force Major, from whose perspective the story is narrated.

While watching the movie, Grandpa fondly told Janet and Lynn how he and Dean Jagger were friends as school-boys in Larwill Public Schools (Larwill, IN - popln 284), especially during high school where Dean (a year ahead of Grandpa) demonstrated enough kindness and courage to become Grandpa's hero and cherished friend. Grandpa spoke with great admiration of his friend. Grandpa also really loved the 1954 film-musical, "White Christmas" with Bing Crosby, where Jagger plays a beloved Major General whose request for reinstatement had just been rejected by the US Army.

Years after Grandpa died, Janet learned that Dean Jagger had gotten his biggest break in Hollywood playing the lead rôle in the 1940-film "Brigham Young – Frontiersman", with Tyrone Power, Vincent Price, and Mary Astor. Janet also learned that Jagger later joined the Church of Jesus Christ of Latter-day Saints based highly on impressions and information he learned while playing the role of the revered church leader, Brigham Young. Janet regrets that she never got to discuss it with Grandpa, but she has a firm faith that she will someday have that hoped-for chat with her beloved Grandpa, beyond the grave.

CUB SCOUTING IN PITTSBURGH.

During Janet's early LDS activity, she was called as the Cub Scout Den Leader for about ten eight year old boys. If that alone weren't enough, Janet's daughters were just five and three years old, and Janet had to bring them along, because John was usually traveling and far too unavailable to watch them. Despite those difficulties, Janet did well enough as scout leader that they kept her in that role for well over two years.

At first, Janet hated how rowdy and impolite the boys always seemed, and she pleaded with the Lord in her prayers for it to end, or for some different behaviors or attitudes from the boys, but it mostly never changed. She did get a strong feeling once that seemed to whisper, "This will give you experience, to better understand your own sons (maybe sons-in-law? Or grandsons?)."

Prior to this calling, Janet had taught the four-to-five year old Sunday school and assisted her good friend, Kathryn Kimball, with her R.S. visits. But, when a by-the-book FBI agent in the congregation was called to be the new bishop, Janet approached him in the hallway.

"You've been on my mind," he said. "In fact, I wrote to Salt Lake about you. You're not a member, but I know that you're doing things. Do they ask you to pray?"

"Yes."

"Well, you can't do that. You just need to tell them, 'I cannot.' Do they ask you to teach?"

"Yes, I teach in Primary."

"Same thing there. I know you go on visits with Kathryn; Same thing there. In fact, since I've heard your husband doesn't like you being here, I will stop by your house this week to ask him about that. Are you doing anything today?"

"Yes, I'm all prepared to teach a lesson in Primary today."

"Well, like I said, you can't do that."

Then, he just walked away, leaving Janet horrified by his pushy and blunt dressing-down, right there in the hallway in front of a bunch of other people.

Janet felt shocked and dazed as she walked to her car. She sat in the parking lot for a long time and began to cry to the Lord, half in sympathy, but half in anger at being treated so harshly and bluntly. A little like Vera so often did to her during her childhood, but she surely never expected it here. If anybody, anywhere ever had a right to be "offended", Janet surely did here at this time and this place.

At first, she thought, "Dear Lord, this has just been way too hard to try to continue this anyway. I'm really done here now." But, then a much stronger and comforting feeling came washing over her. It just doesn't matter. The Savior, Jesus Christ, was treated far worse than this. It just doesn't matter. I'm here because of Him, and nothing else matters.

Three surprising things came from that encounter.

1. That bishop never came to her house and seemed to avoid contact with her after that.
2. Nevertheless, for unknown reasons Janet was immediately called to the Cub Scout calling, which apparently was allowed by the Handbook, even for non-members.
3. Many years later, Janet learned that the bishop had already been secretly involved in serious indiscretions, and would eventually be disciplined by the church soon after Janet and John had moved away to Minnesota. And, that he eventually humbled himself, changed, and returned to honest and genuine service again.

THE LEGACY OF A RELUCTANT CUB-SCOUT LEADER.

Many years later, while living and working in New York, we stopped by the Palmyra visitor center, with my then non-member daughter Anna visiting us from Minnesota. The president of the visitor center was then Edward L. Kimball, son of the former prophet Spencer W. Kimball, and father to Andrew Kimball who was Kathryn's husband.

He told how Andrew and Kathryn now lived in New Jersey, so Janet mentioned having their son Spencer in her Cub Scout den for several years. Edward then briefly shared that Spencer worked for Google, Inc. which was then about to go public through an IPO. Also, if the IPO went as expected, Spencer, then just under thirty years old, was expected to be a millionaire, on paper anyway, given his Google stock options.

Spencer (named after his beloved great-grandfather, the Prophet) later quit Google and started a new company together with two other friends. It took years of difficult struggles, bootstrapping that small startup company and its cloud-based database applications and programs. Nevertheless, today that company (Cockroach Labs) suddenly has a future net worth of over two billion dollars.

Edward was closing for the evening, but asked if we wanted to see the feature film: *"Restoration?"* We said yes, and as Anna watched, she secretly decided to investigate for herself, shortly after she got back home to Minnesota.

Janet and I have repeatedly found hidden blessings in the hardest of struggles. Especially those struggles attached to our investigations and service relating to the Church of Jesus Christ of Latter-day Saints. I certainly could never have written this book without many of those hardest and most long-suffering struggles.

In 1982, Kathryn Kimball was able to obtain multiple copies of the latest printing of the biography, "Spencer W. Kimball" individually signed by its co-authors (her husband, Andrew, and his father, Edward) and personally handled by the aged and infirmed prophet himself. She gave out several copies within their ward, including Janet. Spencer's father was a half-brother (by polygamy) to the famed church general-authority J. Golden Kimball. The book has interesting tidbits on J. Golden, who is notorious for his humor and ability to sprinkle mild vulgarity and profanity into his talks, sermons, and interview-comments. Given Janet's childhood, she has forever since then found a hero and a kindred-spirit in this distant Pioneer relative of the Kimball family, and that autographed book is part of our most prized possessions.

LOST BUT NOT FORGOTTEN.

During Janet's Cub-scout service days, the missionaries presented her with a new program called "set a date" to try to break the gridlock preventing her from being baptized for such a long time. Janet felt somewhat worried that it would not work as well or as easy as they described it. The missionaries understood, but assured Janet that they had already gotten commitments from many in the ward to fast together for this baptism date. Janet agreed and they set the date at March 10th. The four elders gave Janet a blessing, with the most senior companion as "voice". Included were the confident words, "The Lord is mindful of this date, and you WILL be baptized."

They began prayers and fasting ahead of the day Janet was to ask John for permission which was "fast and testimony" Sunday, with the baptism scheduled for the following Thursday evening. John was to catch a plane Sunday evening, and be gone that entire week on business. Janet made John's favorite meal, and took extra-special care in preparing and packing his clothes and suitcase for the trip. He seemed touched and appreciative and when she asked him for permission, she thought he almost said - Yes, before pausing as something then caused his face to harden and he then sneered a simple "No" and left for the airport. Janet agreed with the missionaries to keep praying and calling John each day to lovingly ask permission again. So, Janet faithfully called each day, always getting a No-answer. In fact, Janet could sense an increasing annoyance by Wednesday, so when the missionaries came over to plan and pray for the next day's event, Janet cautioned them. Nevertheless, they agreed to proceed as planned and asked Janet to start calling as early as possible on Thursday and to keep calling until she got the needed Yes-answer. Janet started calling as soon as John was expected to be up that morning, and then kept calling all day at the office where he was at. But John never answered any of those calls, nor did he call back that entire day. Janet checked with the missionaries and found that they had faithfully filled the font and were waiting for her to come with the needed permission. Finally at 9pm, John called Janet back from his hotel and gave his final "No". Janet then quickly called the church where everyone's hopes were crushed, especially the elder who had voiced the confident blessing.

Years later in Minnesota after John moved out as part of the marital-separation, Janet asked her bishop if she could now be baptized. He knew John and worked at the same big industrial corporation, so he said, "No, I think he will come back." That was April. When the divorce papers were drawn in October, Janet asked again, "No - not yet." When the papers were signed in November, Janet was ill and by early December they found the syrinx spinal-tumor. Two brain and spine surgeries got the divorce finalized in court so the bishop said, "Let's get you baptized, does March 10th work for you?" Janet meekly asked, "Why March 10th?" The bishop said, "It's my birthday, and it's the only good fit for your baptism." Janet and the bishop both felt especially amazed as she then related to him the story of the "set a date" episode so many years before in Pittsburgh.

ON MOCKING, AND MOCKERS

Throughout this book I mention mocking and the role it plays in making vulnerable underdogs so much stronger, sometimes even strong enough to defeat the most powerful of forces. Noah was mocked by the entire ancient world around him, for four hundred long years as he quietly built his Ark. But when the floods came and destroyed those mockers, Noah and his family were saved by his patient, courageous, and longsuffering efforts.

Paul was incessantly mocked and mistreated about his supposedly absurd stories, and of his wild-sounding visions on the road to Damascus. Thus he taught the proud people of Athens using their own monument to the "Unknown God". He taught them that he too had mocked, and even persecuted such an "Unknown God" before his marvelous visions, which were so hard for them to believe. But he had seen such visions, and he dared not deny them. Such that no matter what mocking, mistreatment, or even death; he was actually glad to bear it; because Christ (the ultimate "Unknown God"), has born so much more for him, and for all people everywhere in every time and place. Paul's humble patient testimony then grew throughout those people and even to the highest and haughtiest hearts of the mighty Roman Empire until it had gained huge victories over such mocking.

Please do not be offended by my personal comments and opinions. Today we find such mocking and mockers everywhere, even in the church. Especially in the church, so we hope this humble book might be able to help ease some of that growing disharmony.

> *"We live in a cynical world. A cynical world! ...You don't know what it's like to be me out here for you. It is an up-at-dawn, pride swallowing siege that I will never fully tell you about, ok?"*
>
> —Jerry Maguire, *"Jerry Maguire"*, 1996.

Bullying always stops (at least for a while) when "bystanders" combine to carefully document and report it, or maybe even courageously or creatively "intervene" in some other significant way.

CONCERNING "BYSTANDER APATHY", OR DENIALISM OF HARM AND ABUSE FROM BULLYING:

- STOP bystander fear, apathy, and denials of harm and abuse.
- STOP any kind of "by-standing for bullies".
- Intervene, Document & Report them ALL.
    - Always include those closest bystanders.
- Realize that the initial stopping of it is not enough.
    - Accountability and healing that lasts takes more time and effort.
    - Healing is critical for all parties:
        - victims, perps, and closest bystanders.
        - Kindness is free, so "kill'em all with kindness".

REFLECTING

So, if you've read this far, who do you think is most significantly doing the 'KILL' or the "killing with kindness" mentioned in the title; and on the front cover and The Prologue? Likewise, who is doing the most significant and damaging "Mocking"?

Please take some time to reflect back upon the Title, Cover, and The Prologue; Now that you have read the entire book. The power of symbols and metaphor, as discussed in The Prologue, is that they might open up new worlds of considerations and perspectives that you hadn't thought of before.

Janet has often shown me such different symbolic and metaphoric points of view in great literature that we have discussed together, and especially in the Bible, and other great scriptural discussions and teachings. Put yourself or someone you know personally in place of the two cartoon birds on the cover...

Maybe some oppressed minorities, maybe the early pioneers and missionaries, or other underdog refugee groups. Maybe LGBT or other misunderstood minorities. Please try and reflect, and maybe skim back over sections of the book that might help you see it from a different angle, or a different person's perspective. Please always try to never be easily offended, or if an offense has occurred to be open to healing or mending any such offenses.

And, please remember to start writing or recording your own stories, some way or somehow. Also don't forget to help and encourage others in your families to write or record personal and family stories and histories for their posterity and also for the therapeutic value it has for themselves. Anyway, the best "ships" are friendships so, "Cheers to you and me".

PROMOTION AND PROFITS FROM THIS BOOK

Albert Schweitzer, highly distinguished winner of the Nobel Peace Prize and holder of four PhD degrees, sought for years for the basis of a new worldview which could help ease some of the angry divisiveness and polarization happening throughout the world. One day, while in a boat on the river in Gabon, it struck him with great force and clarity: "Reverence for life".

> *"Reverence for Life says that the only thing we are really sure of is that we live and want to go on living. This is something that we share with everything else that lives, from elephants to blades of grass—and, of course, every human being. So we are brothers and sisters to all living things, and owe to all of them the same care and respect, that we wish for ourselves."*
>
> —Albert Schweitzer

In that vein, Janet and I pledge to **dedicate** as much promotion and profits from this book as we possibly can, towards helping those struggling *alone or single*, with any mis-diagnosed -- mis-treated -- or any and every isolated, trivialized, marginalized, *homeless* or misunderstood mental or spiritual struggles. Especially any developmental or other disabilities, eating disorders, mental illness or breakdowns due to PTSD.

GRUDGING ACTIONS FROM BEYOND THE GRAVE.

After this book was submitted for final publication, Janet's father Don recently died peacefully in hospice care. The "Last Will & Testament" mostly refers to a lengthy trust-document originally established in Texas. After Janet and I were married and I insisted that we establish and keep enough distance and boundaries to protect Janet from the damaging stresses her parents kept inflicting, Vera was determined to strike back. She had threatened disowning the girls their entire lives, so after Janet sent the long-letters mentioned earlier, Vera was incensed that they didn't respond to her newest threats.

Vera first recruited Don's only nephew, but after he realized that the entire trust-document was intended to punish and hurt their own daughters, he refused to sign it. Years later while back in Indiana, one of Janet's many second-cousins within Vera's family approached them saying, "My parents are dead, and your daughters are disowned, so maybe we should become family." She knew they had homes, and Cadillacs; and she knew about the Mormon hatred. Thus she was brazenly determined to take advantage.

So, the trust-document got changed, then amended several times. Each time leaving strange inconsistencies and apparent mistakes because of the strange history of its grudging purposes and intentions.

Of course, Janet and Lynn and the three grandchildren were only to receive $1000 each, and if anybody should contest the will or trust they should get nothing according to its dictates. Ironically, years before he died, Don took all investment-accounts out of the trust (for tax purposes) leaving almost no assets there to disperse per the trust-document. At no surprise, the gold-digging second-cousin is currently contesting the will and has frozen all of those investment-accounts. So again we ponder … How-to 'kill' the Mocking Birds?

> "If it be possible, as much as lieth in you, live peaceably with all men. Dearly beloved, avenge not yourselves, but rather give place unto wrath: for it is written, **Vengeance is mine; I will repay, saith the Lord**. Therefore if thine enemy hunger, feed him; if he thirst, give him drink: for in so doing thou shalt heap

coals of fire on his head. Be not overcome of evil, but overcome evil with good."

—Romans 12:18-21.

"I, the Lord, will forgive whom I will forgive, but of you **it is required to forgive all men**. "And ye ought to say in your hearts—let God judge between me and thee, and reward thee according to thy deeds."

—D&C 64:8–11.

WHERE ARE ALL THOSE OTHER SHOCKING UNTOLD STORIES, LIKE THIS ONE?

During Mitt Romney's Presidential campaign-loss of 2012, he surprised some people in getting the votes of many conservative Christian voters who have apparently supported and agreed with the anti-cult, counter-cult, and even the anti-Mormon ministries and literature. Most of the leaders involved in supporting such ministries also refrained to a surprising degree from attacking Romney's campaign, and even supported him, once he won the Republican nomination.

This demonstrates my contention that the main purpose and tactics of these ministries is not really to directly confront the Church, or its strongest members. They find their greatest successes pressuring and punishing the most vulnerable investigators to quit, or to stop their innocent investigations. Most of this pressure is done subtly. They have always somehow succeeded in hiding and denying that it hurts, or has ever hurt anyone.

This book and these stories prove that those gaslighted denials of "not hurting anyone" are a pure hogwash, as to the true stories behind the effects of those ministries. Why has the full story, like this story, never been fully told?

There are plenty of ordinary mocked converts like me, but there are very few stories like Janet's story (it is now much less easily denied, makes for longer-suffering, and includes indisputable damages which have been carefully documented in this book). Janet and people like her are so severely hurt and gaslighted that they are never able to tell or write their full stories by themselves. We need to find them and help them get their full stories told. That is why this book needs to be promoted widely. That is why I am writing it now. Janet and I, together, may be the only ones who can get this important perspective and these stories told, right now. Of course, we need more (we need all) of these important stories, so let's begin here and now.

Many returned-missionaries, over the last sixty years know who these people are. Many of these people never joined the church. But, like our stories, many were repeatedly punished anyway. Many are probably still out there, and maybe are still being punished for investigating, even if they never did join. Maybe this book can somehow reach some of them now?

Please help us reach out to those many other most vulnerable people who have been hurt by the popular opposition discussed in our stories. Please help us gather these stories together so that they can be acknowledged better now. Finally, at this crucial juncture in time, when it is our duty to find a way to gather and get these stories told in a more complete and acceptable way.

So, after reading all of this; How do we 'kill' the Mocking Birds? Kindness is free. Always kill'em with kindness.

"Neither Victims, Nor Fools. Not Ever!"

ENDORSEMENT FOR AN UNKNOWN AUTHOR.

Rather than seek any celebrity endorsement, I would prefer ordinary people who have known me or Janet, to testify about us and/or this book. Please help any future readers know what you think about such things, and why. You can post your thoughts on the following website: www._____ . Does this book have value? Would you recommend it, or anything else by or about me or Janet? Why? Who or how do you think this book might help, in the "real world" today?

"STRUGGLES MAKE US STRONGER,
SO THE BEST IS YET TO BE."